Trends in Schenkerian Research

◆ ◆ ◆

Edited By
ALLEN CADWALLADER

SCHIRMER BOOKS
A Division of Macmillan, Inc.
NEW YORK

Collier Macmillan Canada
TORONTO

Maxwell Macmillan International
NEW YORK   OXFORD   SINGAPORE   SYDNEY

Excerpts from Heinrich Schenker, *Free Composition,* reprinted by permission of Macmillan Publishing Company. Copyright © 1979 by Schirmer Books, A Division of Macmillan, Inc.

Excerpts from Heinrich Schenker, *Der Tonwille* and *Erläuterungsausgabe der letzten fünf Sonaten Beethovens,* by friendly permission of Universal Edition AG, Vienna.

Example 7.1 is from Kirnberger, *The Art of Strict Musical Composition,* by kind permission of Yale University Press.

Schirmer Books
A Division of Macmillan, Inc.
866 Third Avenue, New York, N.Y. 10022

Collier Macmillan Canada, Inc.
1200 Eglinton Avenue East, Suite 200
Don Mills, Ontario MC3 3N1

Library of Congress Catalog Card Number: 89-10937

Printed in the United States of America

printing number
1   2   3   4   5   6   7   8   9   10

Library of Congress Cataloging-in-Publication Data

Trends in Schenkerian research/edited by Allen Cadwallader.
      p. cm.
   ISBN 0-02-870551-3
   1. Schenkerian analysis.   I. Cadwallader, Allen Clayton.
MT6.T75   1990
780′.9—dc20

                                                                                          89-10937
                                                                                               CIP
                                                                                               MN

Contents

Preface

v

Contributors

vii

ONE

Form and Tonal Process: THE DESIGN OF DIFFERENT
STRUCTURAL LEVELS
    Allen Cadwallader

1

TWO

The Compositional Use of Register
in Three Piano Sonatas by Mozart
    David Gagné

23

THREE

Voice Leading and Meter: AN UNUSUAL MOZART AUTOGRAPH
    Larry Laskowski

41

FOUR

Talent and Technique: GEORGE GERSHWIN'S *Rhapsody in Blue*
    Arthur Maisel

51

FIVE

The Development of the *Ursatz*
in Schenker's Published Works
    William Pastille

71

SIX

Rhythmic Displacement and Rhythmic Normalization
    William Rothstein

87

SEVEN

Hidden Uses of Chorale Melodies in Bach's Cantatas
    David Stern

115

EIGHT

Illusory Cadences and Apparent Tonics: THE EFFECT OF MOTIVIC
ENLARGEMENT UPON PHRASE STRUCTURE
    Eric Wen

133

NINE

Handel's Borrowings from Telemann: AN ANALYTICAL VIEW
    Channan Willner

145

Preface

This book is a collection of essays by a recent generation of scholars that incorporates aspects from three areas that have emerged as focal points in Schenkerian research: tonal rhythm, musical form, and motivic structure. These are topics to which Schenker contributed revolutionary insights, but could not elaborate completely during his lifetime. The work here thus extends an analytical tradition, spanning more than five decades since the publication of *Der freie Satz*, that amplifies and develops ideas prefigured in Schenker's writings through the practical application of his approach in diverse contexts. The focus of many of the essays is specific and primarily analytical. Channan Willner, for example, illuminates aspects of musical style through Handel's motivic and rhythmic transformations of Telemann's music; David Gagné relates register and texture to musical form in three of Mozart's piano sonatas.

Readers will also notice the beginnings of general conceptions of these traditional areas of musical inquiry. William Rothstein develops a theory of rhythmic displacement and normalization, and my own contribution explores a more abstract notion of musical form and design at different structural levels. These efforts represent a relatively new trend in Schenkerian research: the development of broader, theoretical formulations that can eventually stand as corollaries to Schenker's theory of tonal structure.

Another trend that has emerged in recent years is interest in Schenker as a figure in the history of music theory, and in the development of his ideas. William Pastille's exegesis of the *Ursatz* concept falls in this category of Schenkerian scholarship and traces the origins of one of the most far-reaching theoretical constructs of the twentieth century.

Unfortunately, it is not feasible in this type of book to include complete musical scores separate from the illustrations. The authors have been diligent in preparing graphs and reductions so that one can hear the music in their examples; I urge readers to seek out and refer to the scores, which complement the illustrations and will greatly facilitate the reading of often detailed analytical expositions.

I would like to express my gratitude to a few individuals whose expertise and advice have been invaluable. First, I extend the warmest and most heartfelt appreciation to Hedi Siegel, who enthusiastically gave of her deep knowledge of Schenker's work and of editing and manuscript preparation; she frequently and patiently advised me on the many details of this project. I am also grateful to my friend and colleague Warren Darcy, who read several of the essays and made many fine suggestions during those times I was working on the manuscript between classes at Oberlin Conservatory. Robert Axelrod, Michael Sander, and Maribeth Anderson Payne of Schirmer Books provided expert support and guidance; John Davis of Music-Book Associates prepared the musical examples and graphic analyses with a consummate artistry that has so beautifully distinguished other publications in music theory. And finally, I offer a special note of thanks to my close and longtime friend Bryson Popham. His friendship, journalistic prowess, and love of music (particularly of Gershwin) were my constant companions through the inception of this project to its completion.

Allen Cadwallader
Oberlin College Conservatory of Music
May, 1990

Contributors

Allen Cadwallader is Associate Professor of Music Theory at the Oberlin College Conservatory of Music. He has contributed articles on Schenkerian theory to *Intégral, Theory and Practice, Music Analysis*, and *Music Theory Spectrum*.

David Gagné is Assistant Professor of Music at Queens College, CUNY, and also teaches at the Mannes College of Music. He has published an article on Monteverdi in *The Music Forum* 6, and an article on Haydn will appear in a forthcoming issue of *Haydn Studien*.

Larry Laskowski is Associate Dean of the Mannes College of Music, where he has been on the faculty since 1977. He has contributed articles to *Theory and Practice* and *The Music Forum* 6, and is the author of *Heinrich Schenker: An Annotated Index to his Analyses of Musical Works*.

Arthur Maisel is a composer and theorist, who has taught at Queens College CUNY and the Mannes College of Music. He has published articles on the music of Ives (cited in *American Grove*), Brahms, and Wagner in *Theory and Practice* and *The Musical Times*. He is also Senior Production Editor for Music in the college book division of Prentice-Hall.

William Pastille is on the faculty at St. John's College, Annapolis. He has contributed articles and reviews on Schenkerian topics to *Journal of the American Musicological Society, 19th-Century Music, Schenker Studies*, and *Theoria*.

William Rothstein, author of the book *Phrase Rhythm in Tonal Music* (Schirmer Books), is Associate Professor of Music Theory at the University of Michigan. He is also active as a pianist.

David Stern is on the Techniques of Music faculty at the Mannes College of Music, and studied Schenkerian theory with Saul Novak, Ernst Oster, Felix Salzer, and Carl Schachter.

Eric Wen is currently editor of *The Musical Times*. He has taught at Goldsmith's College (University of London) and the Mannes College of Music, and has published various articles on Schenkerian theory.

Channan Willner is Acquisitions Librarian at the Music Division of the New

York Public Library at Lincoln Center. He is Editor-at-Large of *Theory and Practice*, having previously served as Editor, and contributes frequent concert and recording reviews to *The Strad*. His publications include analytical studies of performance problems in Handel (*Musical Times*), chromaticism in Haydn (*Theory and Practice*), and the hemiola in Handel's instrumental music (*Göttinger Händel-Beiträge*, forthcoming).

Form and Tonal Process
THE DESIGN OF DIFFERENT STRUCTURAL LEVELS

Allen Cadwallader

> I have repeatedly referred to form as the ultimate manifestation of that structural coherence which grows out of background, middleground, and foreground.... However, within the confines of a book which for the first time seeks to present the concept of organic coherence, the theory of form as a manifestation of the fundamental design must not claim as much space as it would ordinarily find in a separate treatise on form.... However briefly I express myself, I am happy to offer, at least in this manner, the "Essay on a New Theory of Form" which I have promised for decades.

These statements by Schenker occur near the beginning of the final chapter in *Free Composition*.[1] In their tone they proclaim a theory of form arising from his system, a system that describes exactly the principles of diatonic tonal structures. But Schenker's assertions also express a subtle hint of qualification, for as he notes himself, his exposition on musical form is brief. The final chapter in the English edition is only 18 pages long and is accompanied by only nine musical figures in the *Supplement*. Can such an "essay" possibly present criteria sufficiently developed and flexible to serve as the foundation for a theory of form? And if not, does this essay at least illuminate a point of departure and a mode of reasoning consistent with the principles elaborated in *Free Composition?*

One cannot help feeling that Schenker's logic is sound, that he is on the right track when he puts this chapter at the end of his major work. To demonstrate how formal patterns evolve in a particular repertory, one must first understand the repertory's grammar and syntax, its basic constructive principles. And this, after all, is what *Free Composition* is about. In other words, Schenker's methodology, reflected in the evolution of his theories, would not lead him to develop a general theory of form until he had first elaborated the principles of tonal grammar itself.

But Schenker's essay on form is not complete. It remains essentially an introduction, an incomplete outline in need of further elaboration and

1

development.[2] Two points should clarify this assertion, which will emerge clearly as my discussion continues. First, Schenker's outline is too general in most cases; it is based initially on a single premise that leads him to elaborate only the most basic formal patterns. Second—and this is a more significant point—Schenker does not develop and redefine traditional formal principles in light of the central issue in his system, the notion of structural levels.[3]

For example, he explicitly eschews a description of form based on "motive" and does not amplify the significance of concealed motivic repetition in his chapter on form, despite numerous examples in *Free Composition* that show how motives function at different levels in the evolution of formal patterns. The same is true of other conventional terms associated with form. Like motive and harmony, which Schenker elevated to a higher, more abstract plane, the meaning of concepts such as design, contrast, development, and even the notion of form itself, must be reevaluated in the context of hierarchical structures.[4]

I have no doubt that Schenker's system can serve as the foundation for a powerful theory of form if that theory is developed from *within* the framework of his system, and if basic formal concepts are reformulated to reflect the principles of that framework.[5] But it is impossible in a short essay to sketch even the broadest outline for a theory that incorporates and develops Schenker's preliminary ideas. Instead I explore a parallel but more limited topic that enables me to preview aspects of a Schenkerian approach to form without addressing every issue it must embrace. This topic is a hierarchical view of design, the design of different structural levels. Before we explore this notion more thoroughly, however, it will be useful to investigate some of Schenker's ideas about form as they are expressed in the final chapter of *Free Composition.*

Schenker begins his discourse of particular forms with the undivided or one-part form. His lead sentence gives a clear indication of his direction and focus, the basic premise of his approach to musical form: "The undivided progression of the fundamental line generates undivided form."[6] Here we see that division or unity of the fundamental structure is the cornerstone of Schenker's approach: for Schenker, the way in which the fundamental structure is articulated governs formal patterns. Two points shed particular light on Schenker's general line of reasoning here. First, Schenker believed that his initial premise was sufficiently general to apply not just to large-scale form, but also to any level in which a version of the fundamental structure could unfold as an *Ursatz* parallelism. That is clear from the examples of his figure 152, which illustrate formal units ranging from the phrase level to the deepest middleground levels of entire compositions.

Second, this would seem the logical point for Schenker to introduce design as a distinct aspect of form because the formal principle here is so basic (it is simply about the unity of the fundamental line). In discussing figure 152, numbers 3 and 4, he does begin to address design, at least indirectly, when he suggests that immediate repetition of a section, signaled in these cases by a repeat sign, does not alter the unity of an undivided fundamental line and constitute a division of the form. This type of repetition, which might coincide with a division, is conventionally considered a feature of surface design. But for Schenker it is not necessarily divisive for the structure. Thus repetition—a feature that Schenker long believed to be the basic ingredient of form—enters into his discussion, but in this context he refuses to grant it the power to produce form. We shall have to look farther in Schenker's discourse to find repetition of a more articulative nature.[7]

Schenker continues his exposition quite logically, stating that "two-part form evolves most naturally from the division [of the fundamental line]."[8] The interruption procedure is the preeminent issue in this section: interruption leads to a two-part form, but its ramifications are more far-reaching than two complete, lower-level reflections of the fundamental line.[9] Because the goal of the first branch is the dominant, usually with $\hat{2}$ as the main tone in the upper voice, the listener awaits the restatement and completion of the structural descent more intensely than with simpler types of repetition. For the first time in Schenker's outline, repetition enters as a feature of design more articulative than exact restatement within the structure (signaled by repeat signs). Interruption signifies division and recommencement of the structure (as opposed to repetition within a one-part structure). In short, interruption produces a type of repetition that is intrinsically more organic and far-reaching in its application than simple restatement.

In his discussion of three-part song form, Schenker maintains his line of reasoning by stating that "division plays the most important role in three-part form also, even though at the first level it brings binary characteristics to the fore, as a consequence of [an interruption of the fundamental line]."[10] What he means here is that a three-part form can evolve through the *transformation* of a two-part process. Perhaps the most familiar example occurs in cases where a dividing dominant is prolonged as its seventh is worked out in the upper voice; Schenker would say that this is the process of "securing" the seventh. It is, of course, this process itself that articulates and characterizes the middle section at a lower level.

Note another subtle distinction: just as structural repetition was introduced by Schenker as a criterion for a two-part form—either through the complete restatement of a fundamental structure or through its interruption—contrast now emerges in Schenker's scheme. The amplification of a dividing dominant can lead to a separate formal section (for example, a development section) that supports contrasting features at lower levels before large-scale repetition is produced by an interruption. It would seem that two basic ingredients of design—repetition and contrast—are incorporated into Schenker's outline, at least in a very general sense.

Schenker now begins to depart from his basic premise, with its focus on the unity or divisibility of the fundamental structure, acknowledging that "many paths lead to the three-part form."[11] He must admit additional guidelines for the evolution of form because his examples throughout *Free Composition* show that other transformational processes lead to other formal patterns. For example, the mixture of a tone in the fundamental line, the prolongation of a dividing dominant (without interruption), and the working out of a first-level neighbor note are developed as criteria for the evolution of three-part forms. Clearly, Schenker is describing qualities that are less general than the division of the fundamental structure, and that occur at lower levels as unique aspects of design.

This is as far as we need to go in Schenker's essay on form; he uses the basic principles developed in earlier sections to elaborate the sonata, four-part, and rondo forms. But in order to evaluate his brief essay and to indicate how it might be fleshed out and refined, at least preliminarily, it is necessary to state as concisely as possible the essence of Schenker's discussion—some of its irreducible points and their ramifications.

First, one must bear in mind that Schenker's guidelines apply to all structural levels, though this is not obvious at first glance. His examples show numerous lower levels and indicate that he uses the term "fundamental structure" in a broad sense. Often he shows a harmonically closed passage that reflects a lower-level version of a fundamental structure—an *Ursatz* parallelism. Second, Schenker provides sufficient, but not always necessary, conditions for the evolution of certain formal patterns. In other words, at any *given* level Schenker's criteria explain the evolution of basic formal patterns, but he does not describe precisely how formal processes not directly linked to the unity or divisibility of the fundamental line are transformed from level to level. This restricts the scope and completeness of his approach.

Finally, the most fundamental idea that one can extract from Schenker's outline is this: it is *process* that articulates and patterns tonal space, which results in form and design. Schenker raised this issue many times in *Free Composition*, but only tangentially, without qualification or extensive elaboration. Consider the following passage from the chapter on form, in which motion (process) is the central issue: "The development section [of a sonata movement] is primarily a purposeful motion . . . [it] is above all a path, determined by the structural division, which must be traversed."[12] This analogy clearly underscores the dynamic nature of Schenker's conception of musical structure, a quality that must characterize any approach that describes formal relationships in networks of simultaneously unfolding structural levels.

It is now clear that my discussion can take only a first step toward developing Schenker's essay into a theory of form that incorporates process as its first principle. This step explores the notion of design at different levels, and it will indirectly reveal insights about form as a broader construct. Design, of course, is related to form, but its application is often restricted to features that distinguish lower levels. We shall discover, however, that design can also refer to the individual features (the idiomatic tonal patterns) that are generated through transformational processes *at various structural levels* and in ways that closely parallel the evolution of general formal patterns. Consequently, design acquires an abstract and higher meaning, and its application extends far beyond surface and foreground contexts. Schenker stated that "each structural level carries with it its own motives," and I shall claim, in the same spirit, that each structural level carries with it its own form and design.[13]

As I review the properties of traditional concepts in hierarchical networks, a few definitions will clarify my discussion. Process refers to unfolding, to *Auskomponierung.* Progression, which occurs at all levels, signifies the fundamental type of process. In the motion from tonic to mediant, for example, a new scale step is tonicized by a progression that is very general, but one that typifies a smaller class of tonal pieces than does the higher-ranking motion from tonic to dominant. Prolongation is a subsidiary type of process because it usually extends a point within a progression.[14] In this essay, form is defined in the broadest possible way to denote the division, the articulation, of tonal space by process. Finally, design retains many of its familiar connotations, referring to particular features at surface and foreground levels—to texture, registral associations, motivic relationships, changes in local key, the layout of themes, and so forth. But as we shall see, it refers also to features that distinguish all levels below the background.[15]

I have chosen two of Mendelssohn's *Songs without Words* as my examples for several reasons. They are easy to follow with exposition and graphic analyses, and they exemplify many early nineteenth-century formal processes. Moreover, their tonal fabrics are not punctuated by repeat signs or contrasted by marked changes in design at the surface. Initially, I want to avoid addressing the implications of stylistic conventions, such as repeat signs and self-contained B sections in composite forms, so that I may focus on a more seminal issue—the relation between process and the generation of form and design at different structural levels.

Let us begin with an overview of bars 1–10 from the G-major *Song without*

Words, op. 62, no. 1 (example 1.1).[16] This segment is articulated as a separate formal section by a cadence that tonicizes the mediant in bars 9–10 and by a contrasting surface theme that follows. I would also point out that the surface figuration—the accompaniment to the "melody"—is so pervasive and homogeneous that it "smooths over" the formal seam at the surface; below I suggest how this textural aspect of design underscores the formal pattern at the deepest level of the middleground.

Note first the harmonic structure of this segment; a dominant in bar 4 divides the larger motion from I to III into two phrases. A deeper process works across the antecedent phrase, transforming the initial tonic (bar 2) into an augmented sixth (bar 8), which confirms the new scale step of B minor. This is achieved by a linear progression in the bass (in the consequent phrase), which is transferred to an inner voice before it is broken off. The leap to low G reinstates the lower register, thereby clarifying the connection between the structural tonic and the augmented sixth chord in bar 8. Thus far, at least, we see that the way in which tonic harmony is prolonged and transformed is a feature of design because it uniquely characterizes the general harmonic progression I–III. Yet there are also

Example 1.1. Mendelssohn, *Song without Words*, op. 62, no. 1

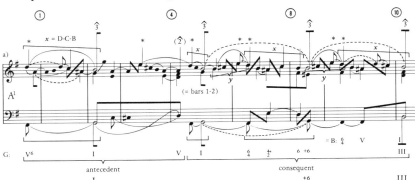

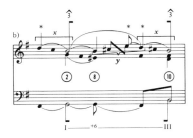

motives that distinguish this passage; because they are expanded in different contexts later in the piece, I shall highlight several of them at this point.

The primary tone $\hat{3}$ is elaborated at the surface and foreground by three interrelated motives that feature the covering tone d². I have given the label *x* to the initial third-progression d²–b¹. The retrograde form of this motive, labeled *y*, reaches back up to d². As we shall see, this configuration recurs in expanded form and counterbalances the descending tendency of the fundamental line. Another motive, d²–e²–d², is more elusive; it hovers like a faint echo above the motives of lower levels. (Its appearances are indicated by asterisks.) This motive conceals formal seams by unfolding across points of articulation and functions as a unifying element in the two-line octave throughout the piece. The second part of the example summarizes these features.

The next formal section is framed by the tonicized mediant in bar 10 and by the first-inversion dominant in bar 22. The dominant six-three, moreover, serves at a deeper level both as the goal of the progression from the initial structural tonic and as the beginning of the reprise. Example 1.2 presents an overview of bars 10–22.

The harmonic and melodic processes that articulate this passage as a formal section are the progression III–IV–V and the descent from $\hat{3}$ to a lower-level $\hat{2}$ in the upper voice. But note also the contrapuntal 5–6 motion that works at different levels and transforms scale steps III and IV, averting the middleground parallels inherent in this bass progression: the 5–6 motion is a feature of design that characterizes this section, at a deeper level, as definitively as the new surface theme that it generates. Furthermore, the expected root-position dominant arrives instead in first inversion. In other words, Mendelssohn leads the bass c of the II⁶ to F♯, the upper third of the dominant, which allows him to return to the opening material of the piece.

More remarkable, however, are the ways in which aspects of design from the A section are recomposed in the process that defines the B section. The first segment supports a linear progression that describes an enlarged version of motive *y* (B–C–D), the counterbalance that reinstates the two-line octave and retards the descent of the fundamental line. But the main point is that the motivic repetition subsumes the new surface theme of the B section, a phenomenon that begins to reveal a richer view of design: a passage whose surface physiognomy is conventionally explained as digression (perhaps through "thematic transformation" of the initial surface theme) actually reconciles repetition and contrast. Hence they are not opposite qualities; rather, each complements the other. Repetition and contrast simultaneously characterize different levels, in a tonal process that articulates a new formal section.

Example 1.2. Mendelssohn, *Song without Words*, op. 62, no. 1

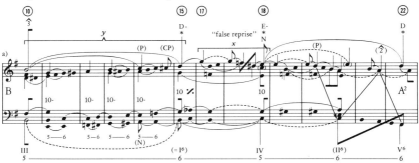

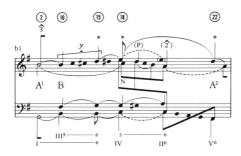

As the transformed mediant moves to the subdominant at a middle-ground level (bars 15–18), d^2 moves to e^2, becoming an expanded portion of the D–E–D covering motive from the A section. As mentioned, this motivic association is most obvious in the two-line octave, and its expansion here provides the tonal environment for a "false reprise," a transposed, subdominant version of the original surface theme.[17] But the process is not complete. As the subdominant is transformed by the 5–6 motion, e^2 descends at the surface to a^1, which prepares a lower-level $\hat{2}$; at a different level, however, e^2 descends conceptually only as far as c^2 (this motion is actually transferred to the bass; see the second part of example 1.2). This reading reveals motions into inner voices, and it means that e^2 is a neighbor note that moves to d^2 at the beginning of the reprise, a motion that completes the unfolding of the D–E–D motive across a formal boundary. The covering motive, consequently, is clarified and brought into sharp focus as it is expanded in a different context, connecting two formal sections in much the same manner as it linked two phrases in bars 1–10.[18]

The function of a reprise, of course, is to recall the context of the beginning—perhaps I should say to recall the tonal process of the beginning. But reprises in the nineteenth century often differ from their Classical counterparts in that variation is frequently incorporated into the final tonic area. In other words, a varied and prolonged tonic region at the end of a composition balances the tonicization of other scale steps in previous sections. Additionally, a prominent feature of design from the initial A section, recomposed in this context, will frequently both confirm and distinguish the concluding tonic area. I conclude my discussion of this piece by focusing on the variation of the original process, specifically, on the extended subdominant region of bars 27–32 in the reprise. Example 1.3 illustrates.[19]

The first phrase unfolds as in bars 1–4, but its dominant goal quickly gives way to a tonic six-three (bar 26) that expands the tonic from bar 24. The subdominant that follows is then prolonged by nested motions into inner voices. As the sketch shows, c in the bass ascends at a deeper level to the chromatic passing tone c♯ (bar 32), which moves to the dominant in bars 33–34. Based on the strength of the expanded subdominant, one can draw a parallel to the harmonic process before the reprise, where the subdominant relates over a larger span—across the mediant—to the initial structural tonic. Here the motion to I⁶ is clearly articulated at the phrase level, but it is subordinate in the higher-ranking progression I–IV–V. The local expansion of tonic harmony is part of the compositional variation of the reprise: it affirms the global tonic, recalling the structural bass motion G–B (I–III) of the initial A section without establishing a new scale step.

Turning to the upper voice, we can see that it is fairly static at one foreground level in the subdominant region. The focus is on the inner-voice tone G, on its elaboration and transference between the one- and two-line octaves. But example 1.3 also indicates more substantive motivic activity at a slightly deeper level.

The main point here is that the upper voice also works out an expanded version of the D–E–D motive. As part of this recollection, a mod-

Example 1.3. Mendelssohn, *Song without Words*, op. 62, no. 1

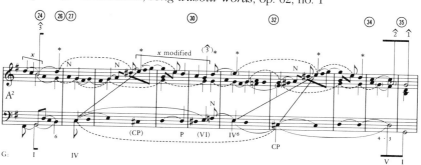

ified version of motive *x* unfolds over the first phrase of the "variation" within the reprise, momentarily reestablishing the primary tone $\hat{3}$, but in a very different context. Thus the reprise exhibits repetition in a conventional manner (the return of the first phrase and the initial surface theme) and in a manner that is variation at a deeper level, in this case the recomposition of the covering motive within the prolonged subdominant region. This more deeply unifying type of repetition both relates and distinguishes the flanking A sections.

The F-major *Song without Words*, op. 85, no. 1, is similar to op. 62, no. 1 in many respects: it also exhibits a cadence on the mediant that articulates the higher-ranking motion from I to V, and the texture is homogeneous, without repeat signs or marked changes in design at the surface. But unlike the G-major piece, a first-level neighbor $\hat{6}$ is worked out as a feature of design that prolongs and elaborates $\hat{5}$ over a large stretch of the middleground, creating a considerable amount of tonal space between $\hat{5}$ and $\hat{4}$ before the fundamental line descends to $\hat{2}$ (this point is clarified by example 1.5). Example 1.4 presents an overview of the initial formal section, which is produced at the second level of the middleground by the progression from I to III.

Although this essay is not primarily concerned with the manipulation and juxtaposition of surface themes, I would point out $\hat{5}$ and the prominence of its upper neighbor $\hat{6}$ (bar 2), which is decorated at the surface by the skip to f². This surface pattern (C–D–F) is embedded within a deeper motive (labeled *x*), a lower-level $\hat{5}$–$\hat{4}$–$\hat{3}$ that governs much of the upper voice of the first phrase; the main line resumes and concludes with $\hat{2}$ only in bars 8–9. Further attempts at closure are thwarted. At the beginning of the consequent phrase, c² again moves into an inner voice, through b♭¹ to a¹, but the line descends no farther. As the dominant of A minor is

Example 1.4. Mendelssohn, *Song without Words*, op. 85, no. 1

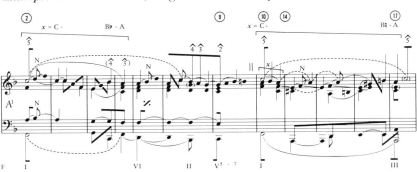

achieved, b♯¹ is established as an upper-voice tone that connects over a larger span the tones c² (bar 10) and a¹ (bar 17) in an enlarged version of motive *x*. Thus two versions of the unsupported stretch unfold in the second phrase: the diatonic pattern is nested within the enlarged repetition, which is altered in accordance with the tonicization of the mediant.

As in the G-major piece, motives from the A section are enlarged and recomposed in a different process that defines a separate section (the B section) and completes the motion to the dominant. Example 1.5 illustrates the tonal structure of bars 17–29.

Once again the progression III–IV–V completes a large-scale harmonic progression from the initial tonic, and once again the 5–6 contrapuntal motion is the voice-leading impetus at a middleground level. As the mediant is gradually transformed by the 5–6 motion, a retrograde version of motive *x* (A–B♭–C, as motion from an inner voice) produces and subsumes the new surface line as it reestablishes the upper register and the primary

Example 1.5. Mendelssohn, *Song without Words*, op. 85, no. 1

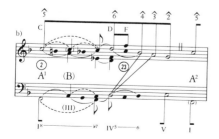

tone $\hat{5}$. As we have seen before, repetition and contrast develop simultaneously: the new surface theme—which introduces contrast (digression) into the pattern of the outer form—derives from the A section as a product of varied repetition at a deeper level. But now a feature appears that provides an additional clue to the distinction between general formal processes and individual aspects of design.

The upper neighbor $\hat{6}$, a deep version of the neighbor note in bar 2, is attained over the subdominant (bar 22). The surface line that emanates from $b^{\flat 2}$ is a slightly altered form of the theme that distinguishes the beginning of the B section, though here it emerges under the influence of $\hat{6}$, not of the primary tone $\hat{5}$. The more remarkable point, however, is that the transformation of the subdominant (by the 5–6 motion) is prolonged at a more immediate level by a lower neighbor A in the bass, which throws f^2 into relief. Thus d^2 "reaches over" at two levels: first to $b^{\flat 2}$ and then to f^2. As the second part of example 1.5 shows, f^2 completes the enlargement of the initial surface figure, c^2–d^2–f^2. This tone succession now spans 23 measures and is one of the deepest manifestations of design we have observed thus far.

The beginning of the reprise presents some analytical problems because of Mendelssohn's dovetailing of formal sections (bars 28–30). A brief glance at the retransition (example 1.5) shows that the upper voice works out the upper neighbor of $\hat{2}$ ($a^{\flat 1}$) as the seventh of the dominant is transferred to the bass, where it functions as a passing tone. The dissonance of the four-two chord increases the momentum of the progression through the formal boundary at the surface, but the expected tonic six-three does not appear. Does the diminished six-five chord that appears instead, which supports the return of the initial surface theme (bar 30), stand for the resumption of structural tonic harmony? In this case I believe it does. Example 1.6 presents my interpretation of the main part of the reprise, bars 30–39.[20]

The upper voice is more straightforward than the bass, a quality that helps clarify the harmonic structure. The primary tone c^2 is active in some sense until at least bar 36 because it is present by contrapuntal implication over the dominant six-five in that bar. But c^2 of bar 37 is the continuation and boundary of the prolonged primary tone $\hat{5}$, meaning that all the descents before this point are lower-level motions, nested x motives, that parallel the similar "attempts" at closure of the upper voice in the initial A section. In this passage we see again the recomposition of a basic premise—an element of design situated at middleground levels—that produces a variation in the reprise. The bass structure seems unusual because the beginning tonic appears in inversion and is transformed by the chromatic passing tone $f^\sharp$, which conceptually originates from an elided f and pro-

Example 1.6. Mendelssohn, *Song without Words*, op. 85, no. 1

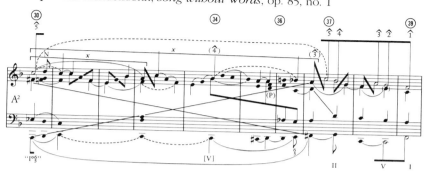

duces the altered "chords" that stand for the tonic and frame its prolongation.[21]

Thus the entire region becomes highly active toward the supertonic, which sets in motion the descent of the fundamental line. I would also suggest that $\hat{3}$ could be read as early as bar 37; this is a plausible alternate reading that would change only the interpretation of the largest version of motive *x* (it would represent $\hat{5}$–$\hat{4}$–$\hat{3}$ of the main line, not a motion into an inner voice). But reading the primary tone $\hat{5}$ prolonged to bar 37 suggests a parallel to the harmonic progression from I to V before the reprise: the descent from $\hat{4}$ unfolds quickly, now near the end of a second process at the first level. This observation is about the design of the fundamental line, about the grouping and rhythmic pacing of its structural tones. But it also shifts my focus to an issue more general than design: the relation between process and the evolution of formal patterns, specifically, the binary form at the first level of the middleground that results from the interruption of the fundamental structure.

I have not included codas in my discussion, a topic that would require a separate study. But because the coda in this piece spans eleven bars out of fifty (bars 40–50), some comments are in order. Schenker did not devote a separate section to the coda in his chapter on form, though he did state that "once the $\hat{1}$ has been reached, a coda section may follow, and there may be a harking-back to the position of the primary tone."[22]

In general, this means that by extending the final tonic after the fundamental line has reached closure, codas provide the tonal environment for recollecting features that unfold at lower levels. In the two pieces discussed here, Schenker's premise describes the circumstances quite well: the primary tones and initial surface motives recur after $\hat{1}$ is attained. But in the F-major piece, versions of the C–B♭–A motive (the *x* motive) unfold at a deeper level, as motions into an inner voice. Once again design is manifested at different structural levels, now in the extension of tonic harmony that defines the coda.

We have seen that the idiosyncratic features and tonal patterns of a composition are transformed through hierarchical tonal processes; design appears at different structural levels. Hence a complete picture of design can never emerge solely from describing surface and foreground appearances (the focus of most conventional *Formenlehren*). These observations reveal parallels to the broader notion of form, because basic formal patterns also derive from tonal processes and characterize different levels of tonal structures. Consequently, a theory of form must be a theory of transformations that traces the evolution of formal patterns as they develop from one level to another. Although the preceding discussion is too brief to support a systematic treatment of hierarchical formal principles, it does suggest the beginning of a Schenkerian approach to form—an approach that describes the evolution of formal patterns through the transformations of general tonal processes that articulate different levels of tonal space.

Consider the first level of the F-major piece. A diagram depicting the two processes (the two branches) is presented in example 1.7, which is based on figure 24 in *Free Composition*. This diagram is very general, but it reveals a division of the structure, a formal pattern, and it indicates that one of Schenker's premises describes perfectly one aspect of the outer form: the interruption leads to a two-part form, but *only at the first level*.

This seems a valid observation about both examples (even in the G-major *Song without Words*, which only approximates the features of an interruption) because of the large-scale motion to the dominant that unfolds before each reprise begins. Moreover, this impression is reinforced by the surface figuration, which smooths over lower-level articulations and changes in surface design to the reprise. Two harmonic-melodic processes at the first level of the middleground—produced by an interruption or a procedure similar to that which underlies the G-major piece—will always impart a two-part quality to the outer form of a composition. And structural *repetition* (signaled by a reprise) is the fundamental feature of design at this level; it distinguishes the beginning of the second process that articulates the structure and reinstates structural tonic harmony.[23]

The form of different levels is highlighted by the design of different levels. In the F-major piece, for instance, the expansion of the surface motive unfolds across the tonicized mediant, underscoring the unity of the higher-ranking progression from I to V that defines a single formal section at the first level before the reprise (example 1.5b). This is evidence for the distinction between form and design. Because the enlarged motive

Example 1.7. Diagram of tonal processes at first and second levels of the middleground

unfolds short of the interrupting dominant, it does not generate a formal pattern. The motive is a feature of design, an *aspect* of the general process (I–V) that articulates the binary pattern at the first level of the middleground.[24]

Example 1.7 illustrates how the outer form develops from the transformation of a tonal process at the first level. The tonicization of the mediant articulates the motion from I to V, producing two sections before the reprise. In all, three formal sections emerge at the second level of the middleground, sections contrasted by the various features of design at different levels. Schenker recognized this "formal dissonance"—the phenomenon of nested formal patterns—when he stated that "division [interruption] plays the most important role in the three-part form also, even though at the first level it brings *binary* characteristics to the fore" (emphasis added).[25] In these pieces a three-part form emerges from the transformation of the binary first level, a view that synthesizes the effects of interactive tonal processes.

These considerations lead me to a tentative generalization about the distinction between form and design: form refers simply to the basic patterns resulting from the articulative effects of tonal processes on different levels of tonal space. Design—also generated through process—is an attendant association and is more specific in its application; it signifies the characteristics of the processes, the physiognomy of the patterns.[26]

These observations also give one cause to wonder if the nature of many divided forms is not intrinsically binary. Schenker believed that repetition was the preeminent element of form. The deepest manifestation of repetition, a reprise or recapitulation, is often produced by an interruption of the fundamental structure at the first level of the middleground: A^1–A^2. From this perspective, the B sections of certain ternary forms could be viewed as an interpolation, at a lower level, that contrasts and therefore amplifies structural repetition: A^1–(B)–A^2. But the notion of an interpolation is metaphorical. In this scenario a B section evolves dynamically from the transformation of one process at the first level into two processes at the second level (before a reprise). Therefore, because an interruption creates form in ways more easily described than those of an undivided structure, the first stage of a hierarchical theory of form can proceed from the study of the implications—at all levels—of the interruption of a fundamental structure.[27]

Finally, since each structural level carries with it its own form and design, a theory of form based on process must accommodate and incorporate in its explanations the interactive processes at different levels that result in an array of forms in a composition. The Mendelssohn pieces, for example, are two-part at one level and three-part at another, though it is more convenient to refer to them simply as three-part song forms. This description is derived from three general tonal processes that are not of equal rank because they do not reside at the same level. Nevertheless, they articulate autonomous formal sections and support highly individual features of design. In short, the label is an amalgam that emerges from describing the effects of interactive processes on tonal space, from illuminating form within form and from the design of different structural levels.

NOTES

1. Heinrich Schenker, *Free Composition*, trans. and ed. Ernst Oster (New York: Schirmer Books, 1979), p. 130.
2. As Ernst Oster pointed out, Schenker "mainly intended to show in broad outlines how the forms, as they appear in the foreground, derive from background and middleground." Ibid., p. 139.
3. I am not aware of any study that systematically lays the foundation for a theory of form based on Schenkerian principles; this study is a preliminary contribution toward that end, reflecting my view that such a *Formenlehre* must be developed completely within Schenker's system. In *Structural Hearing*, Felix Salzer comes close to this view, though

his exposition is essentially an elaborate fleshing out of Schenker's chapter on form. One of Salzer's most useful notions is the distinction between "outer" and "inner" form. In this essay, I use the designation "outer form" for my own purposes, to refer to the design and formal patterns of the first and second levels of the middleground. See Felix Salzer, *Structural Hearing: Tonal Coherence in Music* (New York: Charles Boni, 1952; reprint, New York: Dover Publications, 1962), pp. 220–250 passim.

4. Jonathan Dunsby and Arnold Whitthall argue that "for Schenker, form is not a basic quality of tonal music (or, if so, only of bad tonal music). In a masterpiece, the kinds of formal relationship that had preoccupied analysis throughout the nineteenth century are not, Schenker claimed, fundamental to the musical structure, but are expressed by the structure." See their discussion in *Music Analysis in Theory and Practice* (New Haven: Yale University Press, 1988), pp. 38–40. These statements (and others by Schenker), however, are less about a theory of form than about a philosophical expression of Schenker's world view of musical structure, a view that stands in opposition to many nineteenth-century ideas about music. Though Schenker undoubtedly believed that a new conception of form was latent in his elucidation of tonal coherence, no comprehensive *Formenlehre* is tacitly expressed in his late writings; only an approach and a few principles are adumbrated.

5. Oswald Jonas stated that "Schenker's theory is capable of providing a view of the nature of musical form. [The relevant concepts are] his theory of fundamental structure, which guarantees the unity of the work of art; the fundamental line, which, with its background repetitions, establishes true coherence also in the course of motivic events." Oswald Jonas, *Introduction to the Theory of Heinrich Schenker*, trans. and ed. John Rothgeb (New York: Schirmer Books, 1982), p. 141.

6. Schenker, *Free Composition*, p. 130.

7. At this early stage one might be tempted to criticize Schenker for oversimplifying matters: certainly not all undivided fundamental lines embrace one-part forms. (Perhaps this is why he uses the term "undivided" as opposed to what he later calls two- and three-part forms.) But there may be more to this apparently sketchy and incomplete discussion than is immediately obvious. This and later passages in his essay lead me to a notion that is only foreshadowed in his discussion: tonal processes produce, in different ways, formal patterns at all levels below the background. Here Schenker is describing only the formal consequences—at one level—of the deepest tonal process, the unfolding of an undivided fundamental structure. Hence he does not need at this point to invoke other processes and aspects of design at lower levels that would account for contrasted formal sections within an undivided structure.

8. Schenker, *Free Composition*, p. 132.

9. Schenker also discusses some examples of two-part form in which the fundamental structure is simply repeated. For example, the second section from Chopin's C♯-minor Waltz (fig. 137,1) is two phrases long; each phrase is spanned by a complete descent of the fundamental line at a lower level (an *Ursatz* parallelism). No interruption divides this passage.

10. Schenker, *Free Composition*, p. 132.

11. Ibid.

12. Ibid., pp. 138–139.

13. See Heinrich Schenker, "The Largo of J.S. Bach's Sonata No. 3 for Unaccompanied Violin [BWV 1005]," trans. John Rothgeb, in Felix Salzer and Carl Schachter, eds., *The Music Forum*, vol. 4 (New York: Columbia University Press, 1976), p. 152.

14. These terms are difficult to define in hierarchical contexts and involve unavoidable circularity. Prolongations are realized through progressions at lower levels and, conversely, tonal progressions reduce to prolongations at higher levels. In the most extreme case, of course, all tonal motion stands for prolongation—of the tonic triad. I use these terms in a more practical sense. Progression at any given level refers to the bass arpeggiation, the progression of scale steps that unfolds a triad (for example, I–III or I–IV–V–I). Prolongation is the process by which a scale step is extended in tonal space, from the surface into the foreground and middleground levels.

15. These definitions imply a distinction between form and design, both of which are related through process. Though my observations are primarily about design, a preliminary distinction will begin to emerge as my discussion proceeds.

16. My source for the *Songs without Words* is *Felix Mendelssohn: Complete Works for Pianoforte Solo*, ed. Julius Rietz (New York: Dover Publications, 1975), vol. 2. I would like to express my gratitude to Carl Schachter for his specific insights about aspects of this analysis, and to David Beach, David Lewin, and William Pastille for their insights about this essay in general. Nevertheless, I assume reponsibility for my observations and conclusions.

17. The conditions for this motivic recollection—a false reprise at any transpositional level—would be satisfied in any case in which an applied dominant six-three moves to its root-position "tonic" over the span of at least three bars, as at the beginning.

18. The subdominant of bar 18 functions differently at a deeper level than the description I–III–IV–V might suggest. Because of the covering motive and the "false" reprise, the subdominant is emphasized and is better interpreted as relating directly to the structural tonic of the first

phrase. As the second part of example 1.2 illustrates, the mediant (certainly a goal at one level) is the upper third of a high-ranking tonic. The mediant subsequently is transformed literally by the 5–6 motion into a I^6 at the foreground—the boundary of the tonic region—before it leads to the subdominant. The enlarged half-step motion in the bass (B to C) recalls the similar motion at the beginning (F♯ to G), further corroborating the view that the subdominant is higher ranking than the mediant and underscoring the singularity of the large-scale motion from I to V^6, the significance of which becomes apparent later in my discussion.

19. An interruption does not divide the first level of this piece, though it does exhibit similarities to structures in which the first level of the middleground is interrupted. The V^6 of bar 22 is a feature of design, allowing the reprise to begin with the half-step motion in the bass (F♯–G) that opens the piece; yet this harmony articulates the structure. In other words, there is a sense in which the V^6 is the boundary of a process left incomplete, a process that begins again at the reprise and achieves closure in bar 35. This feature—which is characteristic of a true interruption—underscores the singularity of the harmonic motion to the reprise: the initial process at the first level of the middleground, from I to V^6, divides the piece in two parts. The articulation of this process, by the tonicization of the mediant, produces two sections at the second level before the reprise. This interpretation relates more directly to form than to design, an issue I address briefly in the conclusion.

20. Mendelssohn was a master at introducing large-scale repetition into his tonal fabrics in unusual ways, a technique that can complicate analysis of his music. Sometimes the reprises occur almost imperceptibly as part of a continuous harmonic scheme (see op. 102, no. 4), but just as frequently they signal the return of structural tonic harmony, the beginning of a second large-scale process, though the formal seam and even the tonic chord itself may be concealed. (Schenker, incidentally, sometimes considered unusual manifestations of tonic harmony to stand for structural tonics at points of formal articulation.)

21. Two plausible readings of the deep structure of this piece come to mind. The first (which I have just outlined) is based on the interpretation that $\hat{2}$ over V in bars 25–29 is the goal of an interrupted harmonic progression at the first level of the middleground. The main part of the reprise then exhibits ♯I–V–♯I, a variant of the I–V–I progression over which the unsupported stretch $\hat{5}$–$\hat{4}$–$\hat{3}$ frequently unfolds. In this case the resumption of tonic harmony is concealed (and transformed) by C–B♭–A in the bass, another version of motive *x* (example 1.5). A different reading—and one well worth considering—is that the dom-

inant of bar 25 is prolonged *through* the reprise to bar 38. A definitive interpretation is not necessary for my discussion about design at different levels, but a larger view of the structure figures in my preliminary observations about form. Thus, for the purposes of this essay, I have assumed that the first level of the middleground is articulated by a dividing dominant.

22. Schenker, *Free Composition*, p. 138.

23. We have also seen that a neighbor note can function as an element of design at the first level of the middleground. The consequences of $\hat{6}$ in the first branch of the F-major piece explain the lower-level physiognomy of most of the B section. The climax of the piece ($b^{\flat 2}$), for example, derives from $\hat{6}$ and thus is prefigured in the contrapuntal design of the first level. Furthermore, the deep figure ($\hat{5}-\hat{6}$) takes 22 measures to unfold, revealing a rhythmic dimension to the design of this level. Thus Schenker's statement can be amplified to mean that each structural level carries with it its own motives, form, design, and rhythm.

24. That the first level exhibits a binary pattern is also supported by my interpretation of the deep structure of bars 1–29. The second part of example 1.5 shows that the mediant is subsumed within a higher-ranking tonic prolongation. In other words, the mediant emerges as an autonomous scale step only at the second level of the middleground, where it does articulate a formal section. It is not, however, part of the scale-step progression (the tonal process) that creates form at the first level.

25. Schenker, *Free Composition*, p. 132.

26. We may here consider other meanings and ramifications for terms traditionally associated with design: repetition, contrast, variation, and development. A simple type of repetition occurs when a consequent phrase recalls the thematic material of its antecedent. Likewise, the beginning of a reprise seems to exhibit a similar type of repetition, though we must understand that this type results from an interruption at the first level of the middleground (these types of repetition appear alike because the beginning of the second process [the second branch] at a reprise simultaneously articulates all levels below the background). We have also seen a very different type of repetition—enlarged motivic repetition—that subsumes and produces contrasting features in a different tonal process. It is not farfetched to consider this integration of repetition and contrast as development. Certainly the repetition is developing the pattern of the motive at a deeper level, and this procedure occurs frequently in so-called development sections. Finally, is not this special type of repetition also variation of the pattern? It seems, there-

fore, that viewing design at different levels reveals that these qualities are often aspects of the same thing—repetition, the most basic form-producing procedure.

27. I am currently preparing an essay entitled "Musical Form and the Interruption Procedure."

The Compositional Use of Register in Three Piano Sonatas by Mozart

◆

David Gagné

Registral disposition is one of the most fundamental elements of music. Its role in compositional structure and design, however, has received surprisingly little attention in the analytical literature. The structural implications of register were first clearly expressed by Heinrich Schenker, whose concept of "obligatory register" (*obligate Lage*) was fundamental to his analytical thought. Ernst Oster's outstanding article, "Register and the Large-Scale Connection," describes a variety of structural and motivic relationships that are formed through registral connections.[1] Oster states that "register [is] one of the main elements of composition and is on an equal footing with harmony, counterpoint, and thematic development."[2] He also suggests that register is of particular importance in music for the piano, since "the orchestra, with such a great variety of means at its disposal, does not require the use of register to the same extent as the more poorly endowed keyboard instrument."[3] The significance of register in a composition thus depends not only on structural and stylistic elements, but also on the character of the performance medium itself.

This study explores the role of register in the opening sonata-allegro movements of several piano sonatas by Mozart. I consider not only structure and form, but also melodic and motivic elements, as well as texture, dynamics, and other facets of design.[4] Three sonatas are considered: K. 330 (K. 300h), K. 332 (K. 300k), and K. 333 (K. 315c).[5] Through this comparison I discuss aspects of the treatment of register in Mozart's piano sonatas that are distinctive hallmarks of his style in these works, and reflect the character of the instrument for which they were composed.

Piano Sonata in C major, K. 330

Among the elements that condition the nature of music composed for the piano, two are perhaps paramount: (1) the relatively wide range of the instrument; (2) the disposition of the hands. These elements, moreover, are interrelated. The possibilities for contrast of register that are inherent in the piano (in comparison with a single-line instrument such as the flute that is more limited in range) are vastly enhanced by the performer's two hands, which allow for a multitude of registral effects. The extent to which a composer employs, or does not employ, these registral resources becomes a primary attribute of music composed for the instrument.

In the first movement of Mozart's Sonata in C major, K. 330, the left-hand part occupies a relatively high register for a considerable portion of the movement.[6] This pronounced registral disposition creates a distinctive world of sound that would be difficult to achieve in another medium: it is hard to imagine a string quartet or symphony, for example, in which the lower parts would sustain a comparably high tessitura for such prolonged periods. Because the lower register of the piano is used sparingly, left-hand motions into this register take on considerable sonoric significance and occur most frequently at important structural points. Furthermore, the highest notes in the right-hand part also articulate form and structure over larger spans. (The contrast of registers is more pronounced on Mozart's fortepiano than on the modern piano, enhancing the effectiveness of such structural articulations.) Specific registral associations are most effective on a single instrument, like the piano, by comparison with a group of instruments where timbral contrasts may complicate the perception of registral disposition.

Both hands begin in what may be termed the middle register of the piano. Mozart frequently begins keyboard works in this manner, gradually expanding upward and downward as the piece unfolds. In bars 1–4 the primary tone g^2 ($\hat{5}$) forms an upper boundary in the right-hand part; the arpeggiated figures in bars 5 and 6 thrust upward beyond g^2, reaching c^3, an inner-voice tone that has been shifted above the principal structural top-voice line (example 2.1). The top voice returns frequently to c^3 in the remainder of the first group (in bars 9–10, 12, and 14): this superimposed inner-voice note becomes a boundary or "cover" tone in the first part of the exposition. During the brief transition to the dominant (bars 16–18), c^3 recurs in bar 17, but is now embellished by the note d^3, suggesting an impending motion upward.

The tone d^3, having thus been subtly introduced, emerges as a new high point in conjunction with the structural modulation to the dominant. It occurs in bars 21–22 in association with the neighbor motion D–E–D of bars 19–22, which echoes the G–A–G motion at the beginning of the exposition, consequently unifying the two tonal areas (compare examples

Example 2.1. K. 330, I, first group, bars 1–8

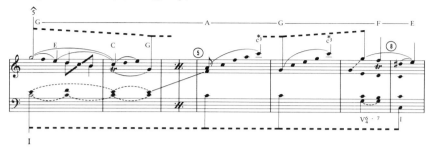

2.1 and 2.2). Further unification is apparent at a deeper level: the right-hand part returns to d³ near the end of the exposition in bars 46 and 52, consequently highlighting a register that forms a registral association between the beginning of the second group and the closing theme.

The relatively high tessitura of the left-hand part is evident from the beginning of the movement. The accompaniment figuration that begins the work is simpler than an Alberti bass, outlining two rather than three voices, but it is similar in purpose. Motions to a lower register emphasize the cadences of bars 7–8 and 15–16, and a new registral expansion to G in the left-hand part (bar 18) articulates and stabilizes the beginning of the second group following the unusually brief transition of bars 16–18.

Subsequent motions below the prevailingly high left-hand tessitura continue to be associated with prominent cadences, as in bars 30–34: here the interruption of the left-hand accompaniment figuration punctuates the texture, serving as an additional form of emphasis. The lower register of the right-hand part in bars 31–34 also enhances the dramatic effect of the passage and intensifies this principal cadence within the second group. Registral changes are frequently associated with variations of texture: the

Example 2.2. K. 330, I, transition and beginning of second group, bars 16–22

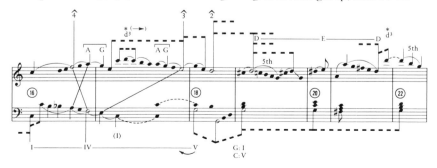

joining of the hands in octaves in bars 38–41, like the solo right-hand texture of bars 34–37, creates a vivid form of registral contrast that makes the lower left-hand part at the subsequent cadence all the more effective. A similar effect is produced by the cadenza-like solo passages in bars 46–47 and 52–53. Thus the registral association of low points, like that of the highest tones, frames the second group. These associations occur throughout the exposition to articulate and unify its internal sections. For example, the low G of bar 18 recurs at the end of the first principal cadence in bar 34 and participates in the last cadence of the exposition in bar 58.

The high left-hand tessitura at the beginning of the development (bars 59ff.) is particularly striking in relation to the preceding low G that marked the end of the exposition. The right hand returns once to d^3 at a point of relative tension, as part of the VII^7 of A in bar 69. This chord ends the 10-measure prolongation of the dominant that begins the development, and initiates a period of relatively rapid motion that leads to the retransition. During the course of the development the left hand does not move lower than the "small" c in bar 76, shortly before the return to the dominant in bar 79 that marks the beginning of the retransition. The change of texture in bars 86–87—that is, the linking of the hands in parallel tenths—constitutes a strikingly effective way of leading to the higher left-hand register at the beginning of the recapitulation in bar 88.

Roger Kamien has pointed out that the recapitulation of a sonata movement is never *simply* a repetition of the exposition.[7] The refinement of Mozart's keyboard style may be observed in the ways in which he varies and recasts the material of the exposition in the recapitulation of K. 330. Shortly after the beginning of the recapitulation a new registral enlargement takes place: in bars 92 and 93 Mozart repeats the figures of bars 5 and 6, but adds additional notes that have not occurred previously in the movement: f^3 in bar 92, and e^3 in bar 93. The specific importance of register in music for the keyboard is evident in the eloquence of this subtle variation. The thirty-second note passage in bar 112 returns to f^3 as the seventh of the V^6_5 chord; the thirty-second note figure in bar 117 reaches e^3, resolving the seventh in that register. Thus the enlargement of the registral space in bars 92–93 is not isolated, but influences the remainder of the recapitulation. Since f^3 is the highest note on Mozart's piano, the movement has now realized the full potential of the upper register, while the predominant left-hand tessitura remains relatively high.

The upper registral boundary of the instrument frequently affects the necessary transpositions of material in the recapitulation. Bars 132–135 have been recomposed since an exact transposition of bars 45–48 would have required the note g^3, which did not exist on Mozart's piano. Bars 129–131 are also recomposed: literally transposing the figuration of bars 42–44 to the tonic would have resulted either in an unsatisfactorily low registral disposition, or in a twofold repetition of the note f³ that would have compromised the climactic effectiveness of e³ in bar 133. The registral characteristics of the piano therefore play a vital role in determining some of the alterations that occur in the recapitulation.

Piano Sonata in F major, K. 332

Mozart's writing for the fortepiano is perfectly suited to the nature of the instrument. At times, however, he employs the medium in a way that seems to transcend its fundamental qualities and dispositions. In the first movement of K. 332, the freedom and variety of textural change achieved by the composer frequently suggest the scope of orchestral writing. This play of textures is closely related to the dramatic use of register.

The work begins, like K. 330, in the middle register of the instrument. In bars 1–4 the hands are linked, despite their rhythmic independence, by a common element of design: triadic motion. The triadic character of the Alberti-bass accompaniment is self-evident; example 2.3 illustrates the triadic structure of the melody in the opening bars and the means by which it is varied through registral displacement.

A radical change of texture takes place in bars 5–8 as the right-hand part continues alone in bars 5–6, answered by the left-hand part beginning in bar 7. The melody and accompaniment texture that had been established in bars 1–4 gives way to imitation: the two hands, which had previously acted in concert, are now juxtaposed. The contrast with bars 1–4 is enhanced by the lower register of the left hand, which reaches F in bar 9, an octave below the pedal tone f of bars 1–5.

In his article "Fortsetzung der Urlinie-Betrachtungen," Schenker comments on the freedom of voice leading in the opening of K. 332. He asks why the melody reaches above the prevailing structural line in bars 3–5 (example 2.3), and offers the following illuminating answers:

1. It makes possible a lighter, freer type of voice leading in bars 5–8.
2. It inspires, mainly, the high notes which are to become the actual high notes of the *Urlinie* in the second 5̂–1̂ succession [of bars 12–22].[8]

Example 2.3. K. 332, I, first group, bars 1–5

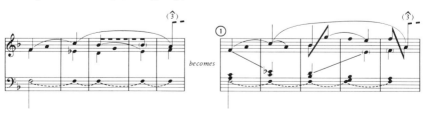

Thus the high register in the right-hand part in bars 3–5 creates an upward momentum that prepares the yet higher register (and the definitive statement of $\hat{3}$) which is reached in bars 12–13.[9] The dramatic change of register represented by the leap to c^3 in bar 12 is reinforced by the left hand, which simultaneously enters the treble register.

These registral changes, together with the rests in bar 12, articulate the beginning of the new phrase, which is associated with an entirely new color and texture. The bell-like sound created by the parallel and similar motion in thirds, fifths, and sixths in the left hand (in the higher register) creates a quasi-orchestral change of color, and suggests traditional horn calls.[10] This radical change of texture and sonority underscores the arrival of the primary tone a^2 in what constitutes the structural (or obligatory) top-voice register.

The harmonic shift to the submediant that begins the transition is underscored by the unison texture of the tripled notes C♯–D in bars 22–23, tones that establish a new low point in the left hand. The dramatic intensity of this moment is reinforced by the *forte* marking, the first dynamic indication that Mozart has notated in the movement. Throughout the transition section (bars 23–40) the sweeps of rising arpeggiation and falling scalar motion in the right-hand part cover considerable ground, but remain within the registral domain established in the first group: as in the first part of the exposition of K. 330, the tone c^3 serves as the upper boundary of the top voice (bars 32, 34, and 36). This tone, however, does not return in the second group, which mainly occupies a lower tessitura. Thus the three-line octave is abandoned until bar 88 in the closing group where the tone c^3 returns. The subsequent rise to e^3 in conjunction with a unison texture (bar 90) marks the end of the exposition with a new registral expansion and a further exploration of this registral domain. Mozart's economical use of the high register at important structural junctures therefore enables him to use it as a frame highlighting and unifying formal divisions.

Commentators frequently describe the opening of the development of K. 332 as a "new" theme.[11] It is true that the thematic material in bars 94–108 has not been heard before as such; nevertheless the theme is closely linked with the preceding material. In general terms, the theme recalls the triadic design that is especially prominent in both the beginning and the end of the exposition. But a more subtle and specific association at a local level suggests that the development continues organically from the exposition: the rising triadic figure g^1–c^2–e^2 in bar 94 echoes the notes g^2–c^3–e^3 in bars 89–90, forming a motivic link with the end of the exposition (example 2.4). Moreover, the contrast between the high register of this figure at the end of the exposition and its repetition an octave lower underscores the sectional division, but does not disrupt the motivic connection.[12]

Example 2.4. K. 332, I, exposition, bars 89–90; development section, bar 94

Example 2.5. K. 332, I, development section, bars 94–132

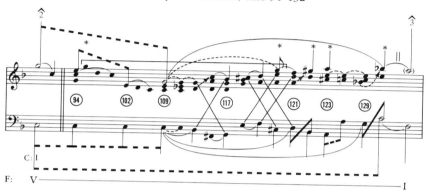

The relationship of the highest tones in the development is closely related to its essential structure, which is shown in example 2.5. The tone g^2 is superimposed above the principal top-voice tone e^2 in the initial phrase of the development (bars 94–101), and is embellished by the neighbor-tone a^2 in bars 99–100. The repeat of the phrase in bars 102–109 is varied through a drop in tessitura; the higher register does not return until near the end of the development, at the point of greatest structural tension, initiating a passage of great wit and subtlety. The tone g^2 returns as a seventh in bar 120, as part of an extended upward motion, and as the boundary of the prolonged (and transformed) C-major harmony from bar 109. After the resolution of the seventh to f^2, the top-voice line moves through $g^{\sharp 2}$ (supported by the augmented sixth chord of bar 122) to a^2 in bar 123. This tone has been of principal importance throughout the movement: a^2 was the initiating tone of the structural top-voice line (bar 13), and it recurred prominently in the transition (bars 24 and 28) and in the second group (bars 45–46, 53–54, and 77–78). The A-major chord with which this tone is associated is then stabilized in a passage (bars 123–126) that is similar to bars 67–70 of the exposition. The chord is heard as a dominant (like the G chord of bars 67–70), and suggests a resolution to D minor, which, however, does not occur. Instead, an A-minor chord arrives in bar 127. The harmonic reasons for this change of quality from major to minor, and its consequences, are as yet unclear. More rests follow in bar 128; then a *forte* chord occurs which clarifies the change. The C^4_3

chord in bars 129–130 is clearly heard as a dominant chord; in reverting to minor, the A chord assumes its diatonic role as mediant. The sudden *forte* has a humorous effect here: having kept us in suspense, Mozart relishes the sudden revelation. The tongue-in-cheek quality of the passage continues as we find ourselves, again following rests, on a root-position dominant seventh chord in bar 131, now at a *piano* dynamic level. The high register of this chord marks the end of the development, and its upper tone $b^{\flat 2}$ is linked through register with the a^2 in bar 123, concluding the large-scale ascent G–G$^\sharp$–A–B$^\flat$ of the development.[13]

The significance of $b^{\flat 2}$ also extends forward. The seventh of the dominant at the end of the development is not immediately resolved in the two-line octave at the beginning of the recapitulation: resolution in this sense occurs only with the arrival on a^2 in bar 145, thus giving to this passage a structural significance that it did not have in the exposition. This connection creates a bridge over the initial theme, forming an organic link that is achievable only through register.[14]

As in K. 330, transformations of registral dispositions play a vital role in the recapitulation. This is particularly true in the final section of the movement, which ends with a dramatic effect through the use of register. As we saw, the highest tone in the work up to the development was the e^3 in the closing section (bar 90) that expanded the high register established by c^3 earlier in the exposition; e^3 occurred as the culmination of the triadic motion between c^2 and c^3, and was followed by a downward leap of a sixth to $g^{\sharp 2}$.[15] In the corresponding phrase of the recapitulation (bars 222–229), the right-hand part moves between f^1 and f^2, then rises through a^2 and c^3 to reach f^3 climactically on the downbeat of bar 226. If the continuation of bar 226 were to parallel bar 90 of the exposition exactly, there would be a subsequent leap up to a^3: this is impossible, however, since f^3 is the highest tone on Mozart's piano. Consequently the upward leap of a third is inverted to a descending leap of a sixth (to a^2), followed by a second leap of a sixth to $c^{\sharp 2}$. The two descending leaps of a sixth isolate F in the three-line octave, dramatically highlighting this register. Thus by attaining the highest point of the tessitura, Mozart concludes the line—defined solely through register—that arches over and punctuates the formal divisions of the movement: in the exposition, c^3 of the first group and transition leads to e^3 of the closing theme, culminating with f^3 in the final bars of the recapitulation, the highest and most conclusive statement of $\hat{1}$.

Piano Sonata in B$^\flat$ Major, K. 333

As we have observed, the middle range of the piano often functions as a normative register in Mozart's piano sonatas, with motions to higher and lower registers taking on structural significance through contrast. At times, however, the middle register may itself assume a referential character, particularly in relation to motivic elements. In K. 333 a motive that begins as an inner-voice motion assumes a primary role in the thematic structure, characteristically in association with the middle register.

The sonata begins, like K. 330 and K. 332, in this central register. The inner-voice tones f^1–g^1–a^1–b$^{\flat 1}$ are divided between the hands, serving as an integral motion that connects the accompaniment and the melody (example 2.6). The figure recurs more rapidly in bars 4–6, again linking the hands.

In the structural top voice, the opening is bounded by the neighbor note g^2. The scalar rise to f^3 in bar 8 suddenly and dramatically opens a new registral domain; the left hand also reaches downward to a new low point, B$^\flat$, in bar 10, strengthening the impact of the cadence at the conclusion of the first group.

In K. 332 the beginning of the transition is dramatically articulated by sonoric, textural, registral, and thematic changes. In K. 333 Mozart minimizes the contrast by beginning the transition (in bars 10–11) with a repetition of the idea that opens the movement. A shift in register occurs, however, serving as a sign that the new phrase has a different structural role.[16] The left hand retains its newly won lower register as the new period begins; the right hand sounds an octave below its first occurrence. Contrast of register, a fundamental resource of keyboard music that is analogous to changes of instrumental color in symphonic works, is frequently employed by Mozart for the articulation of form in these sonatas, as we have seen.

The play of figuration that follows in the transition (bars 11–22) takes advantage of the registral domain opened by the rise to f^3 in bars 8–9. In contrast to the high tessitura of much of the transition, the right hand begins the second group (bar 23ff.) in the same range as the opening of the movement (again illustrating the use of register to articulate formal sections). The motivic rising fourth now occurs in the top voice, transposed to F major as C–D–E–F; the original pattern, F–G–A–B$^\flat$, is simultaneously

Example 2.6. K. 333, I, first group, bars 1–6

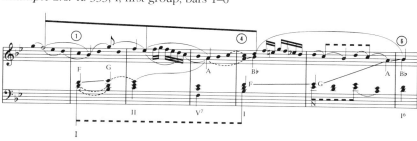

present in its original register (example 2.7). While the first part of the second group is thus relatively contained with regard to register, the rise to b♭² in bar 35 suggests a renewed tendency toward the higher register previously employed in the first group and the transition. As example 2.8 shows, this implication is fulfilled in the subsequent phrase (bars 39–50), where the C–F descent (5̂–1̂ of F major) recurs an octave above the principal register of bars 23–38. The gradual rise in register becomes a dramatic aspect of the design: b♭² is underscored by *fp* accents in bars 39 and 41, while b♮² and c³ are played *forte* in bars 40 and 42. This ascending motion culminates in bar 43 with the arrival of d³, the highest note that has sounded in the second group thus far, emphasized by an octave doubling in the right-hand part and a *subito piano*. The sudden decrease in dynamic level serves as a form of emphasis that is even more dramatic in this context than the preceding *fp* accents and *forte* passages. The octave passage represents a striking break in texture as well as dynamics, marked by the end of the sixteenth-note figuration, and the use of rests in the left-hand part as the octaves first sound. As in the first group, the rise in register in the last part of the second group serves a cadential function in conjunction with the emphatic design elements described above.

Example 2.7. K. 333, I, second group, bars 23–26

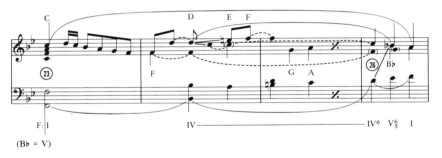

Example 2.8. K. 333, I, second group, bars 23–50

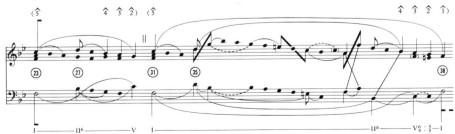

The high degree of continuity characteristic of the movement continues to be evident as the closing theme begins in bars 50–51 with a reiterated, embellished form of the figure F–G–A–B♭ (example 2.9). This motive, it may be recalled, occurred initially in the opening bars; it subsequently appeared in both a transposed and an untransposed version in the second group; finally, it recurs at its original pitch level in the closing theme, even though we are now in the dominant key area. Hence a figure that originated as an inner-voice motive integrates the sections and becomes the structural basis of the closing theme itself.

We have noted that the right hand remained in the middle register in the first part of the second group and then began to climb upward, reaching b♭² in bar 35, c³ in bar 40, and d³ in bar 43. The octaves (d²–d³) in bar 47 return to this tone, linking the high and middle right-hand registers. But the expansion of register continues further in the closing theme: in a triumphant gesture that signals the final structural cadence of the exposition, f³ is reached once again (for only the second time in the movement thus far) in bar 56. The long-range ascent to f³ thus is a primary element of the design that arches over and unifies the second group and closing theme. The intensity of the registral ascent and its culmination in the f³ of bar 56 is underscored by the rhythmic agitation of the prevalent sixteenth-note motion in bars 38–42 and bars 50ff. The play of register is also reflected in the thematic structure: the beginning of the closing theme (bars 50–54) first recalls the middle register of the second group; the rise to f³, culminating the large-scale registral ascent, resumes when the theme is repeated with variation in bars 54ff.[17]

The elements of registral contrast that assume such fundamental importance in the exposition are dramatically juxtaposed in the development. The play of register in its opening bars resembles a dialogue in which both the right-hand and the left-hand parts participate, in a manner analogous to the interchange of contrasting instruments in an orchestral work.

An upward movement in register is initiated by the b♭² in bar 65, the c³ in bar 67, and the d³ in bar 68; this ascent resumes with the dramatic

Example 2.9. K. 333, I, closing theme, bar 50

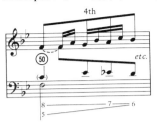

leap of a twelfth to f³ in bar 73, followed by the subsequent motion to e♭³ in bar 77.[18] The arch-like pattern described by these highest pitches concludes with the arrival on d³ in bars 79 and 81. The notes thus emphasized through register are the primary top-voice tones of this section of the development, as shown in example 2.10. The high tessitura returns at the end of the development as the top voice ascends to e♭³, then returns to the lower register to lead to the tone f² at the beginning of the recapitulation.

As in the second group and closing theme, therefore, a conceptually continuous formation—in this case an arch, not an ascent—unfolds over the development. The second (descending) part of the arch may be explained on two levels: the descending motion f³–e♭³–d³ is subordinate to the higher level f³–e♭³, the 8–♭7 of the dominant, which is defined by register (even though the principal register of the seventh is the next lower octave, e♭²), as shown in example 2.11. The register articulates this contrapuntal motion—the second part of the arch—in a way unique to the piece, because it recalls the registral interplay that has spanned the movement.

As a consequence of the transposition of the second group to the tonic in the recapitulation, the motive F–G–A–B♭ now occurs at its original

Example 2.10. K. 333, I, development section, bars 64–94

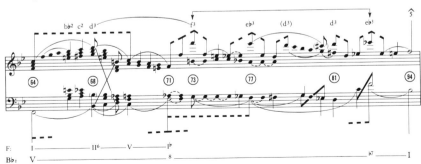

Example 2.11. K. 333, I, development section, bars 71–94

pitch level and register in bars 119–120. In a variation through register that is again analogous to the interplay of different instrumental colors in symphonic music, the consequent phrase (bars 127ff.) is set an octave higher. The brightness of the higher register, in contrast with the darker sound of the antecedent phrase, creates a change of "orchestration," setting off the two phrases from one another in a way that did not occur in the exposition. The brilliance of the high register in the remainder of the recapitulation—and in particular the prominence of f^3—concludes the movement with a focused intensity not unlike the effect of a final *tutti* in a symphony or concerto.

The registral limitations of Mozart's piano may again be observed in bar 162: if the figure at the beginning of the bar were transposed exactly from bar 60 of the exposition, it would rise to g^3, a note not available on Mozart's instrument. One may indeed agree with Eva and Paul Badura-Skoda's statement regarding Mozart's handling of this limitation of range on the fortepiano:

> The apparent ease with which Mozart observed the upper limits of this compass is almost unbelievable. If it should in fact happen that in the recapitulation of a second subject the theme threatened to go above top F because of its transposition into the tonic, the motive would be altered, and in so subtle a way that necessity became a virtue; often this is done in the simplest possible way.[19]

Conclusion

The treatment of register as an element of structure and design in these sonatas reflects not only the consummate skill and subtlety of Mozart's art, but also the specific characteristics of the instrument for which they were composed. Though the range of the Viennese fortepiano was somewhat limited by comparison with later pianos, the degree of contrast between different registers of the fortepiano encouraged the fine timbral distinctions that are fundamental to his style in these works. The influence of the instrument is most evident in the foreground—especially in design elements—but may condition higher levels of structure as well. For example, large-scale registral associations tend to be particularly effective on a single instrument, like the piano, by comparison with a group of instruments where sonoric contrasts may blur registral distinctions.

Mozart's use of the central register as normative in these works enables him to correlate highpoints and lowpoints with important structural junctures.[20] This serves both as a means of emphasis and a way by which the form may be articulated. Moreover, by initially limiting the right-hand register with what I have termed boundary tones, he is able to employ motions to the upper register to highlight large-scale structural relationships, or to create a sense of progression. This technique plays a particularly important role in the development sections of all three sonatas, facilitating the listener's ability to perceive structural connections in the context of rapid harmonic change.

The association of registral contrast with changes in other aspects of design, such as texture, enhances its effectiveness as an articulative device. For example, the octaves in bars 22–23 of K. 332, in conjunction with the downward registral extension in the left hand, dramatically initiate the transition. The joining of the two hands, which normally tend to be relatively independent, is frequently associated with important junctures in the form, as in bars 86–87 of K. 330 where the parallel tenths between the two hands lead to the recapitulation.

The registral and timbral characteristics of Mozart's fortepiano fundamentally condition the character of these sonatas. The sense of progression that is created through gradual registral expansions is an aspect of style that, although possible in another medium, is particularly striking and effective in these works. At times Mozart seems to transcend the fundamental character of the medium: in K. 332, for example, the treatment of register and freedom of texture suggest the scope of orchestral writing. Register may be employed to create a characteristic world of sound in a piano sonata, as in K. 330 where the relatively high left-hand tessitura enables motions into the lower register to assume considerable sonoric import. The disposition of motives with regard to register may be of great significance: in K. 333 the association of the rising fourth-motive with the middle register is essential to the character of the work. Mozart's treatment of register will, of course, vary from work to work, but his use of this musical dimension is a distinctive aspect of style in these sonatas that highlights the articulation of form and structure at various structural levels.

NOTES

1. Ernst Oster, "Register and the Large-Scale Connection," *Readings in Schenker Analysis and Other Approaches*, ed. Maury Yeston (New Haven: Yale University Press, 1977), pp. 54–71. As its title indicates, Oster's article confines itself mainly to large-scale connections established through register, whereas the present study also explores the use of register as an articulative element in the unfolding of form and foreground design.
2. Ibid., p. 55.
3. Ibid., p. 66.
4. The structure is understood as the essential contrapuntal and harmonic framework of the music, while the design is the moment-to-moment realization of the structure in the music itself.
5. The first Köchel number is that given in the original catalog of Mozart's works (Ludwig Ritter von Köchel, *Chronologisch-thematisches Verzeichnis sämtlicher Tonwerke Wolfgang Amade Mozarts* [Leipzig: Breitkopf & Härtel, 1862]); the number in parentheses is the new designation from the sixth edition (Ludwig Ritter von Köchel, *Chronologisch-thematisches Verzeichnis sämtlicher Tonwerke Wolfgang Amade Mozarts*, ed. Franz Giegling, Alexander Weinmann, and Gerd Sievers [Wiesbaden: Breitkopf & Härtel, 1964]). Since the original numbers are more widely known they are employed in this study.
6. The reader is advised to follow the discussion with the music at hand.
7. Roger Kamien, "Aspects of the Recapitulation in Beethoven Piano Sonatas," in Felix Salzer and Carl Schachter, eds., *The Music Forum*, vol. 4 (New York: Columbia University Press, 1976), pp. 195–235.
8. *Das Meisterwerk in der Musik* (3 vols.; Munich: Drei Masken Verlag, 1925, 1926, 1930 [reissued as 3 vols. in 1 slightly reduced facsimile, Hildesheim: Olms, 1974]), vol. 1; trans. Sylvan Kalib as "Resumption of Urlinie Considerations," in "Thirteen Essays from the Three Yearbooks *Das Meisterwerk in der Musik* by Heinrich Schenker" (Ph.D. diss., Northwestern University, 1973; Ann Arbor, Michigan: University Microfilms 73–30626), vol. 2, p. 138.
9. In this analysis, written at a time when his method was still developing, Schenker takes C ($\hat{5}$) as the primary tone; I believe, however, that it is A ($\hat{3}$), as indicated in examples 2.3 and 2.5. The opening bars are not yet clear in this regard, but the top-voice note A emerges as primary in bars 9–12, 13–22, and later.
10. See, for example, bars 13–14, left hand: the intervals third-fifth-sixth as they occur in these bars are typical horn figures.

11. See Arthur Hutchings, "The Keyboard Music," in H. C. Robbins Landon and Donald Mitchell, eds., *The Mozart Companion* (New York: W. W. Norton, 1956), p. 45; and Charles Rosen, *Sonata Forms* (New York: W. W. Norton, 1980), p. 87.

12. Oswald Jonas discusses this type of linkage through repetition ("linkage technique") in *Introduction to the Theory of Heinrich Schenker*, trans. and ed. John Rothgeb (New York: Schirmer Books, 1982), p. 7.

13. David Beach, in his valuable article "A Recurring Pattern in Mozart's Music" (*Journal of Music Theory* 27, 1 [1983]: 1–29), cites the development of K. 332 as an example of the use of the major mediant chord to divide the tonal space between the dominant at the end of the exposition and the tonic at the beginning of the recapitulation. (His figure 6, p. 14, also indicates a prolongation of the dominant through bars 131–132.) I agree with Beach that the A-major chord in bar 123 suggests the possibility of a structural arpeggiation to the tonic; nevertheless, I believe that the C♮ in bar 127 and the subsequent root-position dominant seventh chord in bar 131 effectively negate this possibility. The high register of the left-hand part at the end of the development is consistent with the playful use of register in the movement as a whole, and does not weaken the structural importance of the dominant in bar 131.

14. See Oster, "Register," pp. 61–66, for other examples of such registral bridges that unite different parts of a composition.

This registral resolution unequivocally confirms A as $\hat{3}$, in the obligatory register, in a way that could not occur at the beginning of the piece because there is no "prior register."

15. The tone e³ recurs as a neighbor note in bar 214.

16. The word "sign" is used here in the sense in which it is used by Janet M. Levy in her article "Texture as a Sign in Classic and Early Romantic Music," *Journal of the American Musicological Society* 35 (1982): 482–531. Levy quotes a general definition of the word by Monroe Beardsley (p. 482): "In its broadest sense, in which it can be applied to words, gestures, and semaphore signals as well as markers that direct our way to exits and rest rooms, the word 'sign' denotes any object or event that stands for something else, or leads us to take account in some way of something besides itself" (*Aesthetics: Problems in the Philosophy of Criticism* [New York: Harcourt Brace Jovanovich, 1958], p. 332).

17. Charles Rosen describes the figuration in bars 56–59 as "absolutely conventional," and says that this passage "could be transferred to any work in common time which needs an F major cadence." While the figuration is indeed conventional, the long-range structural importance of f³ and the gradual climb throughout the second group make the significance of this figuration far more than merely "typical." See

Charles Rosen, *The Classical Style* (New York: W. W. Norton, 1972), p. 72. Rosen notes that the passage "provides a climax," but says that it does so "by sounding the first high F in the piece, the top note of Mozart's piano." He is in error here, since the note has already sounded in bars 8–9.

18. The extended falling motion that succeeds the latter two highpoints in the right-hand part is juxtaposed with relative consistency of register in the left-hand part, in contrast to bars 64 (with upbeat) through 70 where both hands participate in the registral play.

19. Eva and Paul Badura-Skoda, *Interpreting Mozart on the Keyboard*, trans. Leo Black (New York: St. Martin's Press, 1962), pp. 11–12.

20. I do not intend to suggest that this treatment of register is always characteristic of Mozart's piano sonatas. In K. 457, for example, he begins by opening up a large registral domain, thereby creating a different set of conditions and implications. Nevertheless it may be said that the element of register plays a central role in the structure and design of all the sonatas.

Voice Leading and Meter
AN UNUSUAL MOZART AUTOGRAPH

Larry Laskowski

A composer's world is essentially a private one. The creative process and musical thinking that lead to a finished work are not generally accessible for study by others, or even by the composer himself. The completed musical work stands alone and is its own explanation and justification. Through performance and listening our intuitive comprehension of the musical discourse and expression grows, and through careful analysis our conscious understanding may increase as well.

Occasionally the composer leaves behind traces of his working procedure that can, if wisely interpreted, provide insight into the composer's thinking. Beethoven's sketchbooks are widely known and have fascinated musicians and scholars over the years. The preservation of such a substantial body of sketches, however, is exceptional. For many composers very little such evidence survives, if it ever existed on paper. Mozart's autographs, for example, are for the most part relatively clean, and the body of surviving sketches is by comparison small.[1] This circumstance has heightened the fascination surrounding Mozart's work, and has contributed to many nineteenth- and twentieth-century popular portrayals of Mozart as the quintessential creative genius.

The autograph of "Bei Männern," a duet from the first act of *Die Zauberflöte*, is exceptional for Mozart because it reveals a major compositional change made apparently during final notation.[2] The autograph, notated in 6/8 time, shows that the placement of the bar lines caused Mozart some difficulty. Mozart seems to have notated two different barrings: the first version begins on a downbeat and continues in 6/8 time to the end. Then Mozart apparently changed his mind, crossed out the bar lines, replaced them with new bar lines shifted by three eighth notes (so that the duet begins in the middle of a measure), and deleted a half-measure of music near the end. The two versions are represented in example 3.1 (melody line only).[3]

41

Example 3.1. Mozart, "Bei Männern," melody line

Such a startling and thorough change relatively late in the compositional process is unusual for Mozart, and commentators have speculated on reasons for the change.[4] In this essay after the chronology of the composition and scoring of this duet are summarized, a brief analysis of the piece is presented and aspects of voice leading, text, and structure are related to Mozart's "last-minute" rebarring.

The text of "Bei Männern," written by the producer and comic actor/singer Emmanuel Schikaneder (the first Papageno and the owner of the theater for which the opera was composed), describes and extols the relationship of man and wife. Mozart apparently took the text quite seriously, for Schikaneder reportedly rejected at least one early version of the music (which does not survive) as too learned and heavy.[5] Schikaneder wanted something light, more in character with the rest of the opera, and perhaps more within his own capabilities on stage. The form of the duet follows that of the text: three sections making an AAB or bar form (or two verses plus an extended coda).

Mozart began intensive work on the opera in April, 1791. Early on he produced a short score, a copy of which was used for vocal rehearsals that summer. Orchestration was begun in early July, and by mid-July Act I (including "Bei Männern") was complete in the full-score autograph that we have today. It is probable that in writing out the full score Mozart's principal task was to orchestrate a reasonably complete short score that had already gone into rehearsal with the singers.[6]

Mozart then turned to other projects and only in September returned to put some finishing touches on *Die Zauberflöte* (the Overture, second-act March and second-act Finale). The premiere took place on September 30, 1791; the composer died on December 5 of that year.

Ascertaining the meaning of a composer's alterations is a difficult task. One can, however, shed light on this fascinating aspect of the compositional process through analysis, which affords a context in which to evaluate the changes. Thus before we begin to explore and interpret the significance of Mozart's rebarring, we shall first examine some specific features of the duet's tonal structure.

The two versions of "Bei Männern" have been aligned in example 3.1; as mentioned, the first version begins on the downbeat, the second on the upbeat. Example 3.2 presents a chordal reduction and a voice-leading graph of bars 1–16.[7]

The first verse exhibits an interrupted descent from $\hat{5}$. The descent is split among three registers, though, and the singers' interplay—their sharing of the descent—is surely related to the partnership described in

Example 3.2. "Bei Männern," chordal reduction and voice-leading graph, bars 1–16

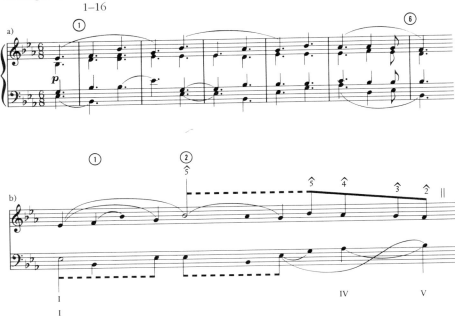

the text. Also, note how the dynamics in bars 12–16 help to highlight the change in register of the upper voice.

Some details of voice leading in bars 4–6 are shown in example 3.3. The essentially contrapuntal E♭-major chords in bar 5 expand the IV–V progression and help to bring the upper voice down to 2̂ from the incomplete neighbor 6̂.[8] The outer-voice voice exchange in bars 8–9 is, I think, quite strong, and necessitates the interpretation of the inner voices shown in the chordal reduction (example 3.2a).

Once one has seen and studied the score, it can be difficult to be objective about the barring. However, I believe that the more natural way to hear bars 1–16 is in barring I of example 3.1, the barring Mozart wrote first but then abandoned. The rhythm of the text itself suggests barring I instead of barring II, and the beginning of the vocal line falls easily at the bar line so that the first measure of the melody consists wholly of tonic. The voice exchange in bars 8–9 is heard more naturally as beginning on a downbeat, the V⁴₂–I⁶ progressions of bars 11–12 are heard as strong-weak, and the final tonic of bar 16 is heard as weak in relation to the preceding dominant.

Two places in the opening 16 measures do hint at Mozart's final barring. In bars 5–6 the motion IV–V from downbeat to downbeat confirms

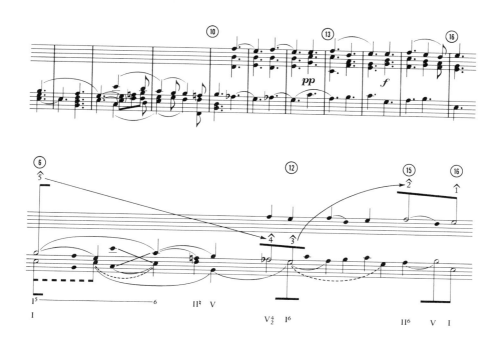

Example 3.3. "Bei Männern," voice leading, bars 4–6

the voice leading shown in example 3.3 (note the bass motion G–A♭–B♭), and in bars 12–13 the bass motion G–A♭ is strengthened by being placed downbeat to downbeat. On balance, though, I believe barring I of example 3.1 to be the more natural way of hearing the opening 16 measures.

The beautiful melodic ornamentation in the second verse does not significantly alter the voice leading or metrical structure from that of the first verse. Our discussion, then, moves directly to the last section of the piece, bar 32 to the end, a chordal reduction and voice-leading graph of which are shown in example 3.4.

The upper voice of this section moves up from the e♭² (at the end of the verse) to b♭² (bar 44), the structural tone $\hat{5}$ in its highest register. (Note the motivic resemblance of the upward motion in bars 32–44 to the ascent in bars 1–2.) A strong structural descent in the high register follows. The only descent in the piece that is unified in register and the only one in this prominent high register, it serves as the culmination of the duet's upper-voice structure. The unity of register, I think, relates to the unity of man and wife, the high register symbolizes the "reichen an die Gottheit an" of the last line of text, and the virtuosic passagework provides a fitting vocal climax. This last section, then, is not just a coda tacked onto a two-verse duet, but a satisfying culmination of musical and textual issues raised in the verses.

Example 3.4. "Bei Männern," chordal reduction and voice-leading graph, bar 32 to end

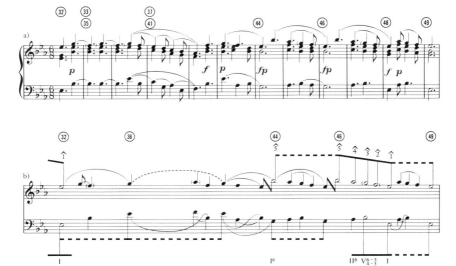

The barring in this last section is very interesting indeed. In my opinion Mozart's final barring in bars 32–43 is, as in the verses, quite unnatural. The $^{6-5}_{4-3}$ progressions in bars 32–36 are inevitably heard as strong-weak; the phrases that begin in bar 36 and bar 38 are heard more easily as beginning on downbeats, not in mid-measure as in the final barring.

In bar 44, though, an abrupt change occurs. Here, for the first time, the final barring (barring II of example 3.1) is unquestionably apt. The placement of the *fp*'s and the measure-long tonic chords in bar 44 and bar 46 confirm the final barring. Note also the progression G–A♭–B♭ in the bass in these bars.

Therefore, a sensitive listener who had never seen the score would not, I think, easily hear the entire duet in a single consistent 6/8 barring. I believe he would hear bars 1–43 in barring I (but would sense conflict and ambiguity from the hints at barring II in bars 5–6 and bars 12–13), and would hear bars 44–49 unquestionably in barring II. In these last six bars all metrical conflicts are undisputably resolved in favor of barring II, and in this climactic passage many other compositional elements come to the fore as well: the highest upper-voice register is achieved, the upper-voice descent is finally unified in one register, the most virtuosic vocal writing is found, the strongest statements of the motive G–A♭–B♭ occur in the bass, and the text "reichen an die Gottheit an" provides the most concentrated image of the central idea of the text. Thus meter is used as one of many compositional elements that promote growth and large-scale shape.

Of course Mozart also faced a less sophisticated problem: to choose a single appropriate barring in notating the duet. It is interesting that Mozart did not choose either of two obvious options, to bar the entire duet in 3/8 throughout, or to insert or delete a half-measure somewhere in bars 43–44 so as to keep bars 1–43 in barring I, and bars 44–49 in barring II. Both of these solutions would have kept the notated and aurally perceived meters synchronized throughout. Instead Mozart tried two other options, barring I for the entire duet, and barring II for the entire duet, both of which involve some disparity between notated and aurally perceived meter.

This is largely a visual issue, but it does seem to have caused Mozart some trouble, and it does relate to musical concerns. The autograph indicates that Mozart's first idea was to maintain barring I throughout. Even though this solution brings the notated and perceived barrings into agreement for the first 43 bars of a 49-measure piece, Mozart eventually discarded this barring, perhaps because it runs counter to his concept of large-scale shape for the piece—that is, culmination and final resolution only in the last six bars. At the climax of the piece this barring scheme abruptly *introduces* a disparity between notated and aurally perceived bar lines. Mozart eventually chose barring II throughout, which instead in bar 44 *eliminates* the disparity between notated and perceived bar lines, and thus reinforces the role of the final six measures as the climax of the piece and the resolution of previous conflicts, even though as a consequence the opening 43 bars are, in this scheme, barred "incorrectly"!

We often point to voice leading, register, text, texture, motives, and themes as elements of music that can be used to promote compositional growth. In a piece's evolution from background to foreground these issues frequently come to the fore and demand attention from performer and analyst alike. Meter, though, we usually relegate to a more static role as a regulator of musical flow, an ordering in time that, while it often can be seen as evolving ultimately from voice-leading factors, plays a more passive role. It is remarkable, then, that in "Bei Männern" Mozart finds a way to allow meter to play an active role in the development of the overall shape of the piece. He accomplishes this within an outward simplicity and consistency, with no notated changes in meter, irregular bars, or tempo changes (within the final version).

Indeed, the surface simplicity of style in *Die Zauberflöte*, the legends surrounding its composition, and the opera's enormous and continuous popularity have all contributed to suggestions that Mozart intended the opera merely as a light crowd-pleaser. Many commentators have correctly countered by pointing to progressive aspects of musical style in the opera. Rosen, for example, argues that the plainness of style represents the culmination of an important historical trend and is characteristic of Mozart's late style, and that "the purity and the bareness are almost exotic, so extreme have they become."[9] Others have pointed to innovative aspects of the orchestration, motivic consistency, and the relationship between music and drama. To the list of noteworthy features we can add Mozart's treatment of meter in the beautiful and deceptively simple "Bei Männern" duet.

NOTES

1. Of course, some sketches do exist, and much can be learned about compositional process from Mozart's autographs. Particularly important among recent studies is Alan Tyson's *Mozart: Studies of the Autograph Scores* (Cambridge, Mass.: Harvard University Press, 1987).
2. A facsimile of the autograph has been published. See W. A. Mozart, *Die Zauberflöte. Eine deutsche Oper in zwei Aufzugen. Text von Emanuel Schikaneder KV 620. Faksimile der autographen Partitur*, ed. Karl-Heinz Köhler (Kassel: Bärenreiter, 1979). The commentary that accompanies the facsimile includes a brief history of the autograph. The first and last

pages of the "Bei Männern" autograph are also reproduced in W. A. Mozart, *Die Zauberflöte*, ed. Gernot Gruber and Alfred Orel, *Neue Ausgabe sämtlicher Werke*, Serie II, Werkgruppe 5, Band 19 (Kassel: Bärenreiter, 1970), pp. xxiii–xxiv. This edition is hereafter referred to as *NMA*.

3. The wind chords in bars 1–2 (full score) are missing in the autograph. Some disagreement exists as to Mozart's intentions in these measures (see *NMA*, xvii), but for the purposes of this essay it is assumed that the wind chords are to be present in bars 1–2 as they are in the autograph in bars 16–17.

4. See *NMA*, xvii–xviii.

5. Otto Jahn, *The Life of Mozart*, trans. Pauline D. Townsend (New York: Cooper Square, 1970), vol. 3, pp. 341–342.

6. A brief summary of the chronology of composition can be found in *NMA*, pp. vii–x.

7. The chordal reductions will facilitate reading this essay without full score. Bear in mind, however, that only the essential foreground structure is provided and that repeated passages are not always written out in full.

8. For similar passages see Beethoven's Piano Sonata in C minor, op. 10, no. 1, II, bars 5–8 and Mozart's Piano Sonata in D major, K. 311, II, bars 1–4.

9. Charles Rosen, *The Classical Style* (New York: W. W. Norton, 1972), p. 321. See also pp. 103 and 319–321.

Talent and Technique

GEORGE GERSHWIN'S *RHAPSODY IN BLUE*

Arthur Maisel

The *Rhapsody in Blue* was first performed in the old Aeolian Hall (on the present site of the Graduate School and University Center of the City University of New York) on February 12, 1924. Despite contemporary predictions to the contrary, it has withstood the test of time, having been with us for over 65 years. Yet the music of Gershwin presents the serious student of music with a problem: there is little agreement on its musical worth. On the one hand, some have found it structurally deficient; Leonard Bernstein, for example, declared:

> The *Rhapsody* is not a composition at all ... [even though] the themes, or whatever you want to call them ... are terrific—inspired, God-given.[1]

On the other hand, Arnold Schoenberg argued for the integrity of the music:

> Many musicians do not consider George Gershwin a serious composer. But they should understand that, serious or not, he is a composer, that is, a man who lives in music and expresses everything, serious or not, sound or superficial, by means of his music, because it is his native language.[2]

That the music has faults is undeniable; still, its merits cannot be gainsaid, even if they are hard to pin down. Both the faults and the merits of Gershwin's music in general—and the *Rhapsody* in particular—have yet to be discussed in any but the most superficial ways, based on gut reactions.[3]

Either to avoid the issue of quality or to treat popular and elite cultures as equal is an all-too-easy evasion—especially in the case of Gershwin, for whom being from the "wrong side of the tracks" was an issue. What is often ignored is that popular and elite artists set themselves different standards. From the point of view of a given set of standards a work made to other standards may seem inferior. Thus, "classical" music sometimes

51

seems dull to the beat- and color-oriented lover of popular music; the lack of words relevant to everyday life is also a drawback.

In any case, Gershwin was aiming to compose according to *elite* standards, despite the popular sources of the musical material (whatever those sources might have been, whether Jewish music, as Charles Schwartz believes, or jazz).[4] In other words, the *Rhapsody in Blue* is an anomaly, for it derives from two worlds. On the one hand, we understand the implications behind Bernstein's comments: the *Rhapsody* sounds like a "composed improvisation," a pastiche of inspired themes and sections that "spill out" spontaneously at every performance. The lack of development of musical ideas (beyond the most superficial kinds of variation) has often been noted; the growth and change we expect in organic musical discourse barely seems to occur at all. These apparent defects in the music reflect the improvisational world of jazz and folk music, the world of the pianists Gershwin pays tribute to in the introduction to his *Song-book*.[5] On the other hand, we can accept the *Rhapsody* on its own terms, precisely because it does belong to this world, far removed from "organic coherence" and the "will of the tones." It is a product of inspired improvisation that does not need to be legitimized through the elite standards of the past.[6]

As I shall demonstrate, however, the *Rhapsody* is more than a succession of beautiful themes and unrelated sections of virtuosic brilliance. It exhibits a coherence comparable in many ways to modes of organization that we associate with the tonal language of the eighteenth and nineteenth centuries. This world, too, was guided by improvisation, for many of the great composers were great improvisers. This is a different order of improvisation—the one that Schenker invoked to explain the long-range "flights of fancy" of a composer—an improvisation able to govern the sophisticated interplay of relationships that unify tonal structures.

The point is that Gershwin's lack of formal training—that is, a traditionally developed *compositional technique*—compelled him to improvise.[7] Improvisation was that aspect of musical composition with which he had the greatest facility: he was, after all, immersed in a jazz and folk culture that thrived on spontaneity. But his great talent also enabled him to grasp, through sheer intuition, the sophisticated compositional techniques of "common-practice" tonality. Thus improvisation of a higher order is also behind the coherence of the structure of the *Rhapsody* on deeper levels. It is the dual nature of its structure, in which apparently unrelated aspects from different musical worlds are juxtaposed, that forms the basis of my discussion.

Through an analysis of the *Rhapsody in Blue*, we can explore the bases of our instinctive reactions, and can better see where the faults and merits of the work lie.[8] The reader should bear in mind, however, that analysis is not the only issue. I highlight unifying interrelationships in the structure of the *Rhapsody*, but often move quickly from surface and foreground to deep middleground levels. This is because my analytical observations serve as a point of departure to introduce and examine briefly a broader philosophical issue: how a talented composer so untrained in traditional composition could write a popular piece that exhibits classical tendencies; in other words, how we might view talent, technique, and improvisation in different ways to explain the anomaly of a structure that derives from apparently unrelated musical worlds.

Bars 1–29: The Source of the Structure

The *Rhapsody in Blue* is certainly an "improvisatory" piece. (That it was in fact *improvised* is also highly probable, as I discuss below.) The act of improvisation can have several stages: the first is often a preliminary idle wandering in which the subconscious has its fullest play. The conscious mind may then decide to consider a certain idea as a beginning, which suggests another idea as it is developed, and so forth. This process guarantees an impression on the surface of continuous invention, a trait that is a common denominator between the two worlds in which Gershwin was composing. But in the classical tradition, the force of improvisation reaches farther.

Put simply, something a bit out of the ordinary (like the C♯ in bar 7 of the "Eroica") will seize the improviser's imagination because it needs to be spun out. It has ramifications that need to be explored and realized—to be "explained." Such spinning out can take many forms, but one apparent characteristic of "higher-order improvisation" is this: the inspired idea, like a seed, holds the potential for further growth and development; it recurs in larger contexts, on grander scales, so that, for example, a simple contrapuntal detail can eventually become the tonality of an extended section.[9] This is what Schenker had in mind when he wrote:

> As a motion through several levels, as a connection between two mentally and spatially separated points, every relationship represents a path which . . . is to be "traversed" in thought . . . the remarkable improvisatory long-range vision of our great composers [is what] I once referred to as "aural flight."[10]

Gershwin's talent—as undeveloped as it was in a traditional sense—enabled him to project improvisation from the foreground into the middleground and background, to engage in "aural flight." This is a remarkable feat; to see how it was accomplished, we must turn to the *Rhapsody* itself.

The opening 29 bars of the *Rhapsody* constitute the unified "inspired core" of the piece, out of which everything else grows.[11] This is shown by both external and internal evidence. As to externals, consider the negative evidence: the manuscript shows signs of hestitation in bars 28–29; furthermore, after bar 29 a solo passage begins on a new page with a slightly different layout, implying a later interpolation. These points suggest that the first section is self-contained, and that after it spilled out at the keyboard, Gershwin was unsure how to proceed.[12]

The theorist is more at home with internal evidence, though here I point out only the salient features. First, referring to the score, consider the opening theme: the first four main notes are B♭–A♭–G♭–F (see also example 4.1a). Now compare the statements of that theme in bars 2–29: it appears first in B♭ in bar 2, then in A♭ in bar 16, and finally in G♭ in bar 21. But the unity of the passage is based on more than the relationship between the main theme and its transpositions: the statements are organized within a circle of fifths, B♭–E♭–A♭–D♭–G♭–C♭ (notated as B), a motion that leads the music to E instead of F.[13] This "overstepping" of the diatonic goal sets the structural agenda, because this foreground motion presents the tritone B♭–E, which underlies the large-scale structure of the piece from the beginning to the so-called "Blues" section (bars 303ff.).

Note also that the main embellishing chord of each of the three statements of the theme contains the dyad E♭–D♭ (example 4.1b). This dyad figures prominently—especially in embellishing chords—throughout the work. For now, I suggest only that this recurring harmonic feature at least makes underlying unity (that is, tonal unity) a possibility.[14] As example 4.2 shows, the surface modulations could be a progression I–♭VII–♭VI in the key of B♭ major-minor, despite the notated key changes.

Finally, note the voice leading of bars 2–27 in example 4.2 and compare it with the voice leading of bars 28–29, which is shown in the second

Example 4.1a. Opening theme, bars 2–4

Example 4.1b. Embellishing chords in first three statements of opening theme, bars 2–23

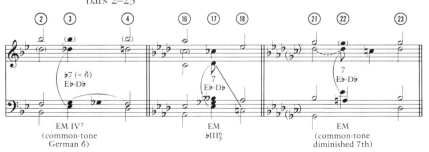

Example 4.2. Middleground graph, bars 2–27; foreground summary, bars 28–29

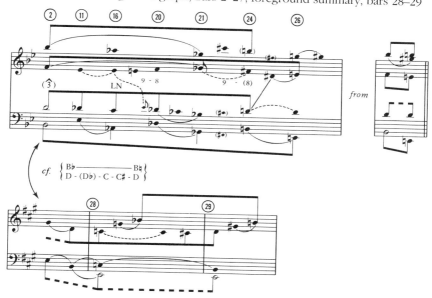

system: the last two bars summarize two aspects of the voice leading that confirm the unity of the entire passage—the inflection of B♭ to B♮, and the neighbor motion D–C–D.[15] Both motions arise in the course of the unfolding of the tritone B♭–E, the structural importance of which has already been mentioned; both motions recur in the piece as unifying elements.

That this passage—the core—is unified is important for two reasons: first, if Gershwin heard bars 2–29 not as three statements of his main theme in three different keys but as a unified structure, it helps to explain why he would recompose certain features to unify later sections and the deeper structure of the piece. This assumption implies the presence of cultivated techniques and modes of organization. Second, because the passage is a point of departure for further development, and because it presents in microcosm the basic premises of the entire piece, we have the means to demonstrate how Gershwin composed a large-scale work, despite his lack of formal training.

A continued examination reveals the relationship between bars 2–29 and the larger structure. Example 4.3 shows that the two important aspects of the background voice leading of bars 2–29 mentioned above—the inflection from B♭ to B♮ and the neighbor note motion D–C–D—are expanded to embrace bars 2–138 (the characteristic dyad E♭–D♭, here spelled E♭–C♯, also shows up in this graph). Example 4.4 compares the deep middleground of bars 2–138 to the structure of the "Blues" theme in E major (bars 303ff.), revealing a sophisticated technique: the voice-leading pattern underlying the "Blues" theme is a transposed, contracted version—a re-composition—of the structural framework of bars 2–138.

Examples 4.5 and 4.6 illustrate in more detail specific aspects of the voice leading and motivic structure of the E-major theme. Example 4.5 shows that the first phrase of the "Blues" theme unfolds within a conventional harmonic framework. Note further, in example 4.6b, the subtle manifestations of the D♯–D–C♯ motive, first heard as part of the opening theme in bar 3 (see note 14); here it elaborates the 5–6 neighbor motion over E in the first phrase. In the second phrase, the motive passes from the "tenor" to the bass (bars 312–313), repeating and transforming the previous 5–6 motion into the descending bass motion E to C♯ in the foreground as preparation for a motion to II.

Example 4.3. Background and middleground graphs, bars 2–138

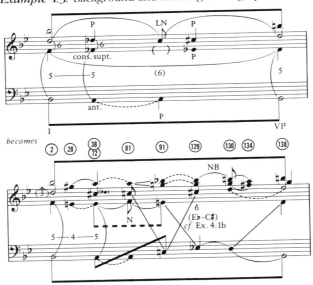

Example 4.4. Voice-leading elements underlying bars 2–29, 2–138, and 303–316 (the "Blues" theme)

Example 4.5. Middleground graphs of first phrase of "Blues," bars 303–310

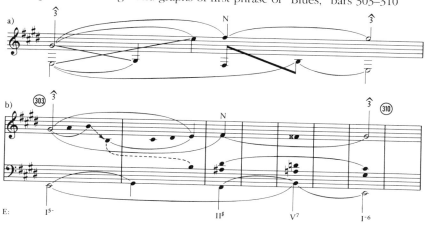

Example 4.6. Middleground graphs of first complete statement of "Blues," bars 303–324

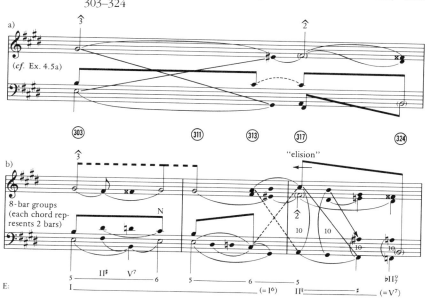

Example 4.7a presents an "abstract" version of the first phrase (the actual music is not shown here), the contrapuntal rhythm of which suggests a straightforward four-measure unit. In the music, however, the F♯ and F× are augmented to twice the value shown (each occupies two measures). Furthermore, the example suggests that the G♯ could function contrapun-

Example 4.7. Four-measure phrase structure of "Blues" theme

tally as the beginning of the second phrase; but in the music, Gershwin brings it in early as the melodic goal of the first phrase. As he did with the F♯ and F♯, he augments the G♯ to twice its expected rhythmic value, thereby completing the rhythmic expansion of the "ideal" four-measure phrase to eight measures.[16] The second phrase is also based on a four-measure prototype (example 4.7b), but it is expanded to only six measures.

That the second phrase is less expanded than the first has to do with the harmony of the third phrase; this can best be explained in connection with the rhythmic augmentation of the inserted G♯ in the first phrase. Referring to example 4.6b, one can see an interesting conflict: melodically, a¹–b¹–c♯² (bars 313–317) apparently constitute a third-progression, but this interpretation contradicts the exchange of voices that prolongs tonic harmony to the end of the second phrase (example 4.6a). In effect, the a¹ (with the passing tone b¹) is an anticipation of the supertonic harmony that begins the third phrase.

The "contradictory" voice exchange of A and C♯ (indicated by broken lines in example 4.6b) can be sorted out by the listener because it participates in an elision at the beginning of the third phrase by anticipating the change in harmony. That the effect of anticipation is heard (despite its stretching over four moderately slow measures) can be explained through the rhythmic force of the inserted G♯ in the first phrase, which helps to expand what is essentially a four-measure unit into an eight-measure phrase: the listener naturally expects eight measures in the second phrase, but the supertonic enters after only six. In other words, the last four measures of the second phrase are set off by the too early change of harmony in bar 317; consequently they can be reinterpreted, in retrospect, as anticipating the third phrase.[17]

We have seen some large-scale resemblances among several sections (and different structural levels) of the piece, but the most striking feature of the *Rhapsody* as a whole is its harmonic structure: a large-scale tritone unfolds from B♭ major of the opening to E major of the "Blues" theme, a motion that derives from the circle of fifths of the opening measures.

Example 4.8 reveals some small-scale motivic connections that underscore the relationship between the B♭- and E-major sections. The neighbor note motion A♭–G♭–A♭ and the chromatic descent E♭–D–D♭ are isolated and transformed in the E-major section *at the same pitch level*. These figures derive from bars 2 and 3, and their presence here suggests that the E-major "Blues" theme is a recomposition of the opening B♭ theme.[18] We cannot know Gershwin's conscious intent here; we do know that the result is a highly refined means of integration.

The tritone's greatest significance is its function in the larger structure of the *Rhapsody*. In bar 29, E, the goal of the circle of fifths, is the dominant of A; but example 4.9 shows that E major—now expanded as a tonal region—operates differently at a deep middleground level. It chromatically prepares the root of an embellishing IV♭7 chord (which again invokes the dyad E♭–D♭). This leads to the conclusion that the two keys a tritone apart represent a single harmonic entity comparable to a I–I♭7 complex in a more traditional tonal context.[19] If such a parallel exists, and I believe that it does, then E major functions as the boundary of a large-scale tonic prolongation and as a kind of applied dominant of the forthcoming IV7.

Example 4.10 compares the opening measures of the *Rhapsody* with its background structure, and summarizes some of the compositional premises that integrate various structural levels. This shows how Gershwin's improvisation enabled him to compose a piece of music akin to the

Example 4.8. Motives retained at same pitch level from opening to "Blues" theme

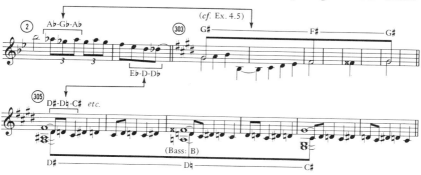

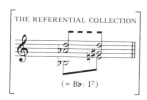

Example 4.9. Deep middleground graph, bars 2–487

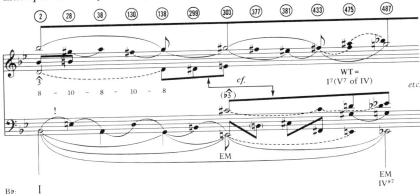

transcendent structures of the classical masters. Note first that the harmonic progression and some of the contrapuntal lines of the first phrase (bars 2–5) have been expanded to provide a framework for the entire piece. An inner voice in bars 2–4, B♭–A♭–G–F, is enlarged to govern the highest voice of the structure. Moreover, we have seen that the E-major theme (represented by an F♭ in example 4.10) establishes a tonal region that is an extension of tonic harmony; example 4.10 shows concisely how this motion parallels, over an enormous span, the expansion of B♭ in bars 2–3, over which the A♭–G♭–A♭ and E♭–D–D♭ motives of the E-major theme first

Example 4.10. Bars 2–5 compared with background structure

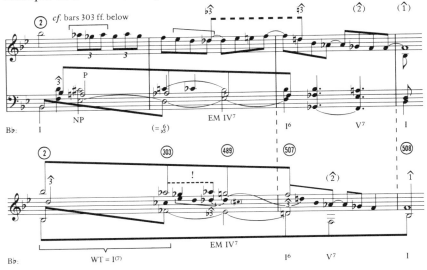

appeared.[20] Finally, the opening theme comes back in B♭ to complete the structural descent: background and foreground *coincide* in bars 507–508.

Gershwin's Technique: Improvisation

Charles Schwartz has convincingly demonstrated that Gershwin composed without benefit of traditional formal training.[21] Given that, it is difficult to explain how he composed with the masterful grasp of tonal relations demonstrated by the instances of untransposed recurrences of motives in transposed contexts, or the unfolding of a structural tritone in a diatonic framework. It is difficult, that is, unless we assume that he had a powerful intuitive grasp of tonal relations. Gershwin seems to have proceeded on instinct; the means he used to tap his intuitive powers was improvisation, for music seemed to flow from his fingers. He once said:

> Sometimes what comes out of that piano frightens me.[22]

But this method of composing has lost standing in recent years, a period when many composers have sought to control their music more consciously than before. Improvisation has become an alternative to composition.

It would be wrong, however, to view composition and improvisation as mutually exclusive. They are, in fact, interdependent. For the musical equivalent of the "willing suspension of disbelief" to occur, composed music must *seem* to be improvised in real time, like the action in a drama. The actor is not really speaking his own mind, but we need to believe that he is. Musical performance requires the same illusion.

But just as composition tends toward an ideal of improvisation, real improvisation can never completely satisfy the condition of composition.[23] In the case of composition, the performer strives to create an illusion of a *successful* improvisation. This can be achieved simply because the composition exists as a potential structure apart from the realization; the performance can be planned. In the case of improvisation, there is a constant underlying anxiety about the whole enterprise for both performer and audience: the structure might fail to materialize. With improvisation, I suspect that the potential for failure rather than the potential for music becomes the center of attention. Thus, while a successful improvisation seems all the more wonderful for having overcome the odds against it, and while it can satisfy musical expectations as fully as the performance of a composed piece, composition provides a more dependable arena for the unfolding and development of musical ideas.

In the *Rhapsody in Blue* the improvisatory origin of the work is revealed in two ways: first, on or near the surface, details suggest their immediate successors. One instance is the gradual emergence of the C-major theme at bar 91 from the material in the bars after 81 (example

Example 4.11. Surface motive emerging from middleground

4.11); such connections result from simple juxtaposition, an obvious hallmark of improvisation. The second way that improvisation reveals its presence is that the large-scale structure of the piece is also prefigured by local detail. Recall, for example, the tritone motion that eventually governs a large stretch of the deep middleground. It seems unlikely that Gershwin planned even the more superficial instances of such relationships, and even more unlikely that he was aware of the deeper ones.

Compositional structure seems to have meant repetition for Gershwin; he constantly reworked the same material with only the most elementary variation and no surface development to speak of. The weakest features of the structure are precisely those in which he seems to impose the most conscious control, evincing a lack of traditional training. Hence the unification of the *Rhapsody* over larger spans is the more remarkable. It can be explained only by assuming that Gershwin possessed a talent, an intuitive understanding of higher-order improvisation.[24]

Talent and Technique

The analysis of the *Rhapsody in Blue* allows us to "watch over the shoulder" of a talent both mature and relatively untrained. It also thus raises the vexing issue of the relationship between talent and technique, the issue, in other words, of what part of a composer's ability is innate and what part learned. In one sense, this problem is exacerbated in Gershwin's case by the imbalance between his enormous talent and his unrefined technique. In another sense, however, this very imbalance gives us the opportunity to consider separately qualities that are not usually separable. To explore the implications of this complex aesthetic issue is beyond the scope of this essay; it can, however, suggest ways in which Schenker's ideas contribute to an area of musical inquiry not typically associated with music analysis.[25]

In any description of the roles of talent and technique in the compositional process, the two factors, though in fact inextricable, must be examined separately. For this I propose the following working definitions: talent is a profound, intuitive understanding of the relationships between pitches and between rhythms, relationships that shape and extend through all structural levels. Technique, developed through training, is the craft of musical creativity. It enables the composer consciously to manipulate the materials of music and to create a surface impression of cohesion. This distinction agrees with one's feeling that even composers sometimes found deficient in their handling of larger structures (for example, Schubert and Chopin) are talents of the first rank.

The talent of the composer does not lie in a faculty that others do not possess, so much as in having "more" of that faculty—the way some people are taller than others. The point here is that just as no amount of exercise can *increase* one's height (though one's athletic ability, for instance, can be developed), no amount of training can create a talented composer. This conclusion seems obvious when it refers to the classical masters. It is all the more so for Gershwin because the deficiencies of his foreground sharply contrast with his ability to create an integrated large-scale structure.[26]

Schenker's theories support the thesis that talent applies to large-scale structure and not just to surface detail. Musical talent is unitary; it extends through all dimensions of compositional process because the pitch structure itself is unitary (deriving ultimately from a single pitch and its overtones). There is an aspect to this subtle point—so central to Schenker's thought—that is often overlooked because attention is concentrated on the multiplicity of levels: not only is the pitch structure unitary in its horizontal aspect of being the expression of a single tone in time (as is widely understood), it is also unitary in its vertical aspect: all structural levels coexist in the foreground.[27]

In the case of the *Rhapsody in Blue*, one aspect of musical talent, improvisation, allowed Gershwin to create a unified structure despite his lack of compositional training at the time. (It would be of interest to study his more consciously crafted later pieces to see what effect, if any, greater control had on their success.) We begin to see how these results tend to confirm the a priori nature of musical talent, and how such findings are implicit in Schenker's theory of tonal music. The unity of the pitch structure means there is no such thing as talent that applies only to the foreground: the impact of talent extends fully into all dimensions of musical structure.

But it also means that the average music lover's ability to apprehend the foreground is not different in kind from an ability to apprehend the background. If this is true, then the current state of affairs in which the composer and listener have nothing to say to each other must end soon. For neither the intensification of craft nor the dissolution of content can guarantee communication. Rather, both composer and listener must rely on their common heritage, the irreducible musicality of human beings.

NOTES

1. Leonard Bernstein, "Why Don't You Run Upstairs and Write a Nice Gershwin Tune," in *The Joy of Music* (New York: Simon & Schuster, 1959), p. 57.
2. Arnold Schoenberg, "George Gershwin (1938)," in *Style and Idea*, ed. Leonard Stein (New York: St. Martin's, 1975; reprint, Berkeley: University of California Press, 1984), p. 476. First published in *George Gershwin*, ed. Merle Armitage (New York: Longmans, Green, 1938), p. 97.
3. Exceptions are Charles Schwartz, *The Life and Orchestral Works of George Gershwin*, (Ph.D. diss., New York University, 1969), on which his book, *George Gershwin: His Life and Music* (Indianapolis: Bobbs-Merrill, 1973) is based; and Stephen E. Gilbert, "Gershwin's Art of Counterpoint," *Musical Quarterly* 70, 4 (1984): 423–456.
4. Schwartz, *Gershwin*, pp. 321–333. It ought to be expressly stated that despite its having been improvised, the *Rhapsody* is not jazz. In this connection, and with reference to what I was saying about the distinctions between popular and elite art, note that jazz has sometimes been called "America's classical music." I think this characterization is apt not only because jazz is a serious artistic pursuit, but also because it strives toward a "classical" balance between repetition and development: recall that, in addition to being improvisatory, it is also based on *variation*. Like European "classical" music, jazz has demotic sources but is not really demotic music in itself.
5. *George Gershwin's Song-book* (New York: New World Music, 1932). Reissued in part (by the same publisher) as *Gershwin at the Keyboard* (n.d.).
6. It seems to me that all music involves a balance between the predictable (literal repetition) and the unpredictable (growth or change), and that different types of music can be distinguished by their different ways of balancing these elements. Western elite music has valued the unpredictable: literal repetition is considered less artistic than varied repetition; *hidden* repetition, which integrates the unpredictable with the predictable, the most artistic. Popular music, in contrast, is quite comfortable with literal repetition; consider its strophic forms—and, on another level, its emphasis on the beat. The unpredictable element tends to be more concentrated: take, for example, what is known in

contemporary popular music as the "hook"—or, in relation to the repetitive beat, the more pervasive use of intense syncopation.

That some of these considerations might have been in Gershwin's mind is demonstrated by the music at bars 81–89, where a self-consciously serious "developmental" passage (including canonic imitation) is followed by a bright jazzy tune (bars 91ff.) that seems to poke fun at the foregoing seriousness. An essential feature of this tune is that it *seems* to come out of nowhere—it is also never heard again (see example 4.11).

7. Gershwin was not only a habitual improviser, but in this case was forced by circumstances to work especially quickly. Schwartz (*Gershwin*, pp. 74–95) carefully reconstructs the actual course of events in the composition of the *Rhapsody* from the sort of legends that seem early on to have become attached to Gershwin.

8. The analysis is from my dissertation, "Talent and Technique: George Gershwin's *Rhapsody in Blue*" (Ph.D. diss., City University of New York, 1989).

9. See Felix Salzer, "Haydn's Fantasia from the String Quartet, Opus 76, No. 6," in Felix Salzer and Carl Schachter, eds., *The Music Forum*, vol. 4 (New York: Columbia University Press, 1976), pp. 161–194.

10. Heinrich Schenker, *Free Composition*, trans. and ed. Ernst Oster (New York: Schirmer Books, 1979), p. 6.

11. Table 4.1 (p. 66) is provided because no measure numbers appear in the score. The layout refers to the two-piano "original version" that I have used for my analysis (New York: New World Music, 1924).

12. The manuscript score is in pencil and consists of 56 pages. The parts ("Jazz Band" and "Piano Solo") are written in the usual two-piano format seen in reductions of piano concertos. The manuscript can be seen on microfilm in the Library of Congress, call number "Music 1350."

13. The a^{b2} in the B^b-major context might be viewed as motivating the inception of the descent through the circle of fifths. I do not find this a completely satisfactory explanation of this passage, however, because the A^b is heard here as the seventh *step* of the parallel minor mode in mixture with the major tonality of B^b. Schwartz (*Gershwin*, p. 296, n. 32) relates the succession of key changes to Gershwin's habit of frequent modulation when improvising at the piano.

14. Note that the motive in bar 3 of example 4.1a, e^{b2}–d^2–d^{b2}—an elaboration of the dyad E^b–D^b—is significant for drawing connections between the opening measures and the "Blues" of bars 303ff.—as is the triplet figuration a^{b2}–g^{b2}–a^{b2} in bar 2. The motive is introduced as f^2–e^{b2}–d^2–d^{b2}, but the first note can be detached for four reasons. First, it figures more importantly in the initial motive b^{b2}–a^{b2}–g^{b2}–f^2. Second, the F–E^b–D–D^b figure is "answered" immediately by E^b–E–F, suggesting that a

Table 4.1
Correspondence of Page Numbers and Bar Numbers in the *Rhapsody in Blue.*

Page	First bar on page	Page	First bar on page
2	1	23	230
3	19	24	236
4	31	25	243
5	41	26	260
6	48	27	276
7	60	28	289
8	70	29	303
9	78	30	327
10	88	31	339
11	97	32	350
12	106	33	370
13	115	34	391
14	124	35	411
15	138	36	429
16	147	37	441
17	162	38	455
18	171	39	469
19	181	40	481
20	196	41	494
21	206	42	501
22	215		

three-note rather than a four-note motive is involved. Third, it is in its three-note form that the motive recurs throughout the piece. Fourth, the E♭–D–D♭ motive is a melodic form of the E♭–D♭ dyad, which is an interval in the local harmonic goal. (Strictly speaking, in Schenkerian terms, a motive usually unfolds an interval of the prevailing harmony. What I am calling a motive is really submotivic diminution. Unfortunately, there is no other term besides "motive" to refer to diminution that is consistent throughout a piece.)

15. The 9–8 suspension in bar 24, which highlights the inflection of B♭ to B♮, is implied by c♯³ in the flute part while the piano arrives on B in the bass; note that bars 19–20 show the same suspension explicitly (a step higher).

16. The expansion was probably introduced to allow the D♯–D–C♯ motive to unfold at the level of two measures (as shown in the "tenor" of example 4.5b) through its syncopated reiteration on the surface, as shown in example 4.8.

17. Compare the melodic anticipation of the supertonic harmony coinciding with the chromatic inflection of the tonic on the last quarter of bar 5 in the first movement of the "Hammerklavier."

    Another factor works in conjunction with the asymmetrical rhythmic structure of the phrases, contributing to the effect of anticipation and elision. It is unusual for the tonic in a Classical phrase to be prolonged by a neighboring 5–6 motion, such as occurs over eight bars in the first phrase of the "Blues" theme; such a motion raises instead the expectation of a change of harmony to the supertonic. The change of harmony, however, is denied at the beginning of the second phrase, which begins again with tonic harmony. The denial of expectations arouses one's "anticipation" (in the general nonmusical sense), but the first supertonic one hears (in bar 313) turns out to be within the tonic prolongation. Having considered it as a possible fulfillment of one's expectations, though, one tends to connect it to the real supertonic that comes in bar 317.

18. The interrelationships of the B♭ and E passages are most beautifully underscored at bar 356 where E♭–D–D♭ is transformed into a reference to the A♭–G♭–A♭ motive. If there is something haunting about this embellishing chord (containing the dyad E♭–D♭, of course), it is because we have heard it before—one of the first things we heard, in fact—in the second half of bar 2.

19. For this reason, I find it especially significant that the two linking motives involve the notes A♭ and D, respectively—that is, the tritone in common between the seventh chords of B♭ and E.

    The referential collection shown in example 4.8, besides encompassing two dominant seventh chords a tritone apart, is also a whole-tone collection—the same composed out in bars 475–486 (see "WT" in example 4.9).

20. The arrival on the deep-level IV⁷ in bar 489, recalled from bar 3, is signaled by a theme (not shown) that features the dyad E♭–D♭ prominently. This is significant because the theme was first heard in bars 11–14, at the beginning of the circle of fifths that established the tritone as a structural interval.

21. Schwartz, *Gershwin*, pp. 52–56.

22. Quoted in Oscar Levant, *A Smattering of Ignorance* (New York: Doubleday, Doran, 1940), p. 232. Given to the Gershwinesque character, Sam Frankl, in the play *Merrily We Roll Along* by Kaufman and Hart (Act 2, Scene 3).

23. This assertion has been questioned by Carl Schachter, who cites great composers like Bach, Mozart, and Beethoven as improvisers (private communication). First, I think that it is fair to assume that even such masters had better and worse days as improvisers. Second, I am at-

tempting here to describe *phenomenologically* the differences between composition and improvisation; I do not doubt that any number of Mozart's improvisations were more successful as musical structures than any number of compositions by Salieri.

24. Of course, Gershwin wrote the piece in a matter of two to three weeks; he did not have the leisure to sketch or otherwise carefully construct his first major instrumental work. The legend, probably true, has it that he forgot his promise to Paul Whiteman to write a piece for the band until very shortly before the deadline. It is at least plausible that the reason he forgot was that he knew he would be improvising anyway. Perhaps, unconsciously, he hoped to legitimize his compositional method by putting himself in a situation where it was the only possible way to proceed.

25. This section touches on some broader philosophical ideas that arose during my study of the *Rhapsody*, ideas that were treated more fully in my dissertation (see note 8 above). Here, I simply want to preview a possible future essay that will enable me to discuss in detail the philosophical implications of my work.

26. My position cannot be fully set forth here, but I want to prevent one possible misinterpretation if I can. One might conclude from the discussion that I think talent per se is innate; I do not. I think it is reflexive in much the same way that reading is.

Schenker posits a Hegelian dialectic between art and nature as the ground of the synthesis that the tonal system represents—and I agree. In this view, the dialectic is reenacted in various relationships in every piece of tonal music; examples are the relationship between tonic and dominant and that between tonality and diatony (loosely, melody). The distinction between talent and technique is implicit in the dialectic in that, through technique, a composer fashions what nature provides in the form of a pitch and its overtones, while talent is what allows the composer to grasp what nature provides and what can be done with it. Talent is thus a heightened form of the musicality that probably *is* innate in all people.

27. Schenker, *Free Composition*, p. 18. In a manner of speaking, the "timeless" unity of the pitch in nature is expressed moment to moment by the vertical aspect of polyphony. In the synthesis that we call "music," the antitheses of timeless pitch and unfolding in time (or rhythm) are involved in a dialectic—and are renamed "harmony and counterpoint."

Linguistic models of tonal music fall down on just this point of vertical unity: there is no background apart from what is present (either literally or by strong implication) in the *foreground of the music itself.* In contrast, the Chomskyan background structure of a sentence often disappears in the process of transformation, except for traces left in the foreground. Thus, in Schenker's approach, the background of a piece of music is not reconstructed from the foreground so much as it is laid bare. At any rate, the superficial resemblances between Chomsky's levels of structure and rules of transformation, and those of Schenker, should be understood as artifacts of analysis. It bears repeating that Schenker was a superior music theorist because he grew more and more to think of music *as music:* the graphs are music— not words, not pictures, not anything else.

The Development of the *Ursatz* in Schenker's Published Works

William Pastille

The *Ursatz* is something of an enigma. In order to feel comfortable working with it, we academic Schenkerians have done our best to demystify it. We have become quite content to think of it as a "theoretical construct," or as a "hypothetical substructure," or as an "axiom." In other words, we speak of the *Ursatz* in terms that sound scientific, perhaps because the atmosphere of science has a reassuring bouquet of scholarly rationality about it, or, at any rate, because we breathe it more easily than the atmosphere of organicism, life forces, and the will of the tones. But when one reads *Free Composition*, one cannot escape the sense of mystery that surrounds the concept of the *Ursatz*, nor can one ignore the impression that something essential is slipping by unnoticed. This impression arises, at least in part, because in *Free Composition* we encounter the *Ursatz* as a fully formed, mature, and independent idea; but, of course, the *Ursatz* had a history—it developed out of Schenker's analytical studies gradually over a period of years. In this paper I attempt to trace that growth process and, by catching the *Ursatz* in its genesis, so to speak, to grasp some of its elusive qualities. I try to tell, in brief outline, the story of the *Ursatz* concept in Schenker's writings, from its beginnings to its emergence as a fully formed idea.[1]

Tracing the origins of an idea is usually a difficult task. Ideas have a tendency to spring up in the company of similar or related ideas, and it is often impossible to disentangle the roots of one idea from those of associated ideas. In the case of the *Ursatz*, however, Schenker himself indicated the starting point for our inquiry, as we shall see. The development of the *Ursatz* concept begins in the first volume of *Counterpoint* (1910), with the notion of *melodic fluency*—a principle, Schenker says, of

71

shaping melodic lines so that successions of large leaps are avoided. This is accomplished by interspersing melodic seconds and thirds between such leaps, or by reversing direction in a second leap, or by both of these means in combination.[2] He cites, for instance, the opening theme (bars 1–18) from the Adagio of Beethoven's Ninth Symphony as an example of melodic fluency at the surface level: in that melody, even leaps as small as a fourth are recovered by means of a second, a change in direction, or both.[3] But the principles of melodic fluency need not be slavishly maintained on the music's surface; many angularities and disjunctions may appear at the surface level if one or more guiding lines beneath the surface exhibit melodic fluency. Examples 5.1 and 5.2 show such guiding lines: example 5.1 reveals a line which is, as Schenker puts it, "the ultimate product of ascending and descending figurations" in the Prelude from J. S. Bach's D-minor English Suite;[4] example 5.2 shows three separate, melodically fluent contrapuntal voices underlying a polyphonic melody from a later point in the same piece.[5] These two examples demonstrate that two sorts of results may be expected when the principles of melodic fluency are operative beneath, rather than at, the musical surface. First, long-range melodic relationships—such as that shown in example 5.1—may come to light. Second, underlying contrapuntal patterns—such as that shown in example 5.2—may become apparent.

In the years following the first volume of *Counterpoint*, as Schenker began to delve more and more deeply beneath the musical surface, the two abilities afforded by knowledge of the principles of melodic fluency—namely, the ability to uncover long-range melodic motions and the ability to reveal underlying contrapuntal patterns—became the mainstays of his analytical approach. In fact, the further development of his work can be

Example 5.1. Bach, English Suite VI, Prelude, bars 1–15 (Schenker)

Example 5.2. Bach, English Suite VI, Prelude, bar 165 (Schenker)

charted by following the progress of the interaction between these two analytical abilities.

During the decade of the teens, Schenker published four books, all dealing with works of Beethoven: the analysis of the Ninth Symphony (1912) and the analyses of the Piano Sonatas opp. 109, 110, and 111 (1913, 1914, and 1915, respectively). These works are, in the main, thematic analyses; that is, one of their principal aims is to demonstrate the coherence that pervades the succession of thematic and motivic events at the surface level. Nevertheless, Schenker does occasionally make use of the notion of melodic fluency to establish overarching melodic motions or underlying contrapuntal patterns. Two instances of the latter are shown in examples 5.3 and 5.4, in which Schenker explains the functions of two unison passages by referring them to their underlying contrapuntal contents: in both cases the unison pitches of the musical surfaces (in bar 25 and bar 39, respectively) are interpreted as simple passing tones in the underlying counterpoints.[6]

In the next two examples, a similar process occurs in two stages: first, in example 5.5, Schenker diagrams the melodically fluent activity beneath the actual music; then, in example 5.6, he derives the content of the last three bars from an underlying contrapuntal passing motion in the sketches marked *a*, *b*, and *c*.[7] At *a*, the e^{b2} of the upper voice passes between f^2 and d^{b2}; at *b*, it is accompanied by the c^{b2} of the inner voice; and finally, at *c*, a $^6_4$ construction delays the arrival of d^{b2}.

Example 5.3. Beethoven, op. 109, III, var. 2, bars 24–26 (Schenker)

Example 5.4. Beethoven, op. 110, I, bars 38–41 (Schenker)

Example 5.5. Beethoven, op. 111, I, bars 5–10 (Schenker)

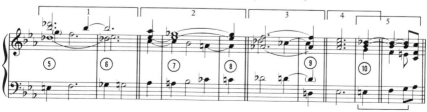

Example 5.6. Beethoven, op. 111, I, bars 8–10 (Schenker)

While it is characteristic at this stage in the development of Schenker's thought for underlying contrapuntal patterns to span only a few bars, the identification of underlying melodic motions tends to reach somewhat farther. Example 5.7, for instance, shows a long-range, descending melodic line traversing the entire 19-measure development section of Beethoven's op. 110, I.[8] Obviously, this line is fairly close to the surface of the music— it is not at all difficult to match the tones of the sketch with their counterparts in the score. But the real power of melodic fluency to reveal underlying melodic coherence begins to appear when Schenker applies the principle *twice* to the same passage of music. Example 5.8 shows this process in action.[9] From bars 41–48 of the score, Schenker derives the melodically fluent descending lines shown at *a*; then, by seeking the melodic fluency underlying those two lines, he uncovers the neighboring motion shown in the first system at *b*. By following a similar procedure for each of the three succeeding eight-measure phrases, Schenker is able to trace the melodic line through the 32-measure section. It is out of this very powerful technique of applying the principles of melodic fluency repeatedly that the next stage in the evolution of the *Ursatz* concept arises—the discovery of the *Urlinie*.

The years 1916 through 1919 saw no publications by Schenker, but immediately following this hiatus the notion of *Urlinie* appears for the first time in the analysis of Beethoven's op. 101 (1920). Although Schenker does not define this term, expecting the reader to infer its meaning from the analytical sketches that accompany his commentary, he does provide it with an ancestry that allows us to trace it back to the principles of melodic fluency. After introducing the term, Schenker says that he is now going to discuss the concept in rather more detail than he could when he first

Example 5.7. Beethoven, op. 110, I, bars 38–56 (Schenker)

Example 5.8. Beethoven, op. 110, II, bars 41–72 (Schenker)

hinted at it in *Counterpoint* I, and he cites precisely the discussion of melodic fluency that yielded examples 5.1 and 5.2, as well as the instance of the opening of the Adagio from Beethoven's Ninth Symphony mentioned earlier.[10] It is clear, therefore, that Schenker himself viewed the *Urlinie* concept as an outgrowth of the principles of melodic fluency. Indeed, an examination of the analytical sketches that accompany the op. 101 commentary discloses the activity of the same principles we observed in the earlier sketches, except that the range of their application has now been greatly expanded. Example 5.9 shows two analytical sketches that map out the content of a passage from Beethoven's op. 101, II.[11]

A comparison of the score with the sketch labeled *Ausführung* reveals that Schenker has recorded melodically fluent versions of the several lines making up the setting. In the lowest line, for instance, the octave leaps in the score are smoothed out, resulting in the predominant movement by seconds that is characteristic of melodic fluency. Similar principles resolve all the other lines into motion by seconds as well. Having attained in this sketch a melodically fluent version of the whole setting, Schenker proceeds, in the sketch marked *Urlinie*, to clarify the contrapuntal origins of the setting. For example, the direct chromatic successions at the start of the lower line in the *Ausführung*—not permitted in strict counterpoint—are shown to derive from a purely diatonic line in the *Urlinie* sketch, and then the motion in parallel sixths above that line stands out more clearly. Or, to isolate just one more instance, the accented passing tone g^2 on the downbeat of bar 5 of the *Ausführung* sketch is shown to have originated as a simple passing tone in the same bar of the *Urlinie* sketch. These sketches show the two main sources of melodic fluency—long-range melodic relationships and underlying contrapuntal patterns—acting in consort as Schenker probes the space below the music's surface. Incidentally, the many brackets in these sketches demonstrate that at this stage in the development of Schenker's thought the notion of concealed motivic repetition was already in place; the brackets here indicate the repetitions of

Example 5.9. Beethoven, op. 101, II, bars 1–8 (Schenker)

the descending fourth-motive introduced at the outset, and of the derivative third-motive first introduced in bar 4.

At the same time, however, Schenker was also reaching even deeper levels of melodic coherence by repeatedly searching out the melodic fluency of a single passage. Example 5.10 shows this procedure.[12] The sketch at *e* is a melodically fluent version of the score, which is actually very ornamented and disjunct. Sketches *d*, *c*, *b*, and *a* depict successively more fluent versions of the upper line of sketch *e*. Step by step, the reversals and disjunctions of the line in sketch *e* are resolved, until a single, melodically fluent, arched line in seconds remains at sketch *a*.

At this time, Schenker was using the term *Urlinie* to refer both to high-level lines such as that in sketch *a* of example 5.10 and to lower-level lines such as those in the *Urlinie* sketch of example 5.9. The possibility of confusion that might seem to arise from this equivocal nomenclature seldom causes difficulty, however, because the context of Schenker's analytical commentary almost always makes clear which of the alternatives is intended.

Procedures of the same sort as those just examined continue to exert their influence on the analyses of the first few issues of *Der Tonwille* (1921 and 1922). I have said elsewhere that the first of Schenker's analyses to be explicitly informed with the notion of complete organic coherence seems to be the essay on Mozart's Piano Sonata, K. 310, which appears in the second issue of *Tonwille* (1922).[13] But it took Schenker some time after that to develop a notation that could convey this sense of overall coherence. Example 5.11 shows one of the earliest and least complex instances of such a notation: it comprises two sketches published in *Tonwille* 4 (1923).[14] The large sketch in this example is a measure-by-measure, melodically fluent version of the actual music, somewhat in the style of the *Ausführung* sketch of example 5.9, except that the lines are on a higher level. By this time, however, Schenker was calling such sketches as this *Urlinie-Tafeln*, and he had started to use the term *Ausführung* to refer to the music as it appears in the score. Nomenclature aside, the advances of this notation are in the use of the capped, arabic scale-degree numerals and in the use of different-sized noteheads; for now Schenker can show both the melodic fluency of the measure-by-measure motions and the long-range melodic fluency represented by the scale-degree designations. In addition, the scale-degree numbers help to orient higher-level sketches, such as those at *b* and *a*, to the *Urlinie-Tafel*. If the simplicity of the sketch at *a* comes very close to the simplicity of the later *Ursatz*, this may be explained partly by the simplicity of the actual music. All the same, within just a few months Schenker was to introduce virtually all the remaining conceptual elements that would lead to the fully developed conception of the *Ursatz*.

Example 5.10. Beethoven, op. 101, III, bars 1–20 (Schenker)

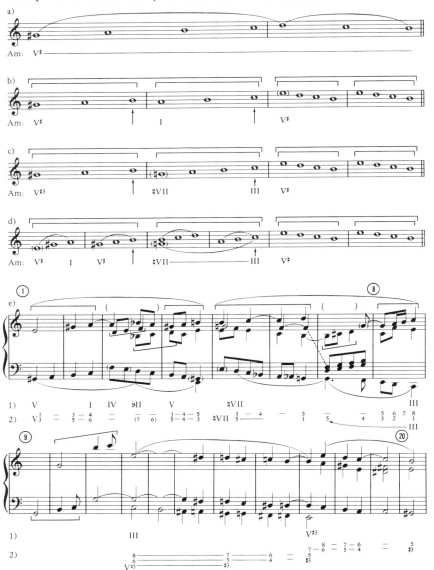

Example 5.11. Bach, Twelve Little Preludes, no. 2 (Schenker)

Later in 1923, in the fifth issue of *Tonwille*, Schenker published the graph reproduced in example 5.12.[15] In this example, one can see the two principles of melodic fluency taking their place within the incipient framework of Schenker's fully developed analytical technique: the characteristic motion by seconds is prominent at all levels of the graph; the identification of underlying contrapuntal patterns is apparent to the eye as one glances up from letter *f* toward letter *a*; and the great notational advance of aligning different versions of the sketch vertically makes the concerted action of the two principles all the more visible. Glancing downward from *a* toward *f*, on the other hand, one can clearly see how the extremely simple counterpoint of letter *a* is expanded both by the motion in seconds of the melodic linear progressions, and by the more and more elaborate contrapuntal patterns of succeeding levels. These increasingly more elaborate conceptual extensions of the voice leading, which Schenker now calls *Stimmführungsprolongationen*, henceforth become the principal focus of his analytical method.

In connection with the same example, Schenker introduces for the first time the term *Ursatz*. "At *a*," he writes, "one can see the *Urlinie* tones in a two-voice *Ursatz*. One can undoubtedly consider this setting [*Satz*] as a bit of a deviation from a voice leading based on a real *cantus firmus*; the materials available here would be too scanty for a *cantus firmus* setting. But in any case, the purity of the interval successions corresponds to the requirements of strict counterpoint."[16] While this passage does not define the term *Ursatz*, the use of the word *Satz* in the context of strict counterpoint clearly suggests that Schenker intends *Ursatz* to mean "setting of the *Urlinie*." Since the *Urlinie* in this instance is the music's most comprehensive melodic line, then its contrapuntal setting, its *Ursatz*, is the music's most comprehensive contrapuntal model. Here in the *Ursatz*, at

Example 5.12. Bach, Twelve Little Preludes, no. 5 (Schenker)

the highest level of abstraction, we see the ultimate unity of the two principles of melodic fluency. Whatever mysterious connotations the word *Ursatz* might take on later, it retains its essential meaning: it is the strict contrapuntal setting of the most comprehensive melodic line in a piece of music.

On the whole, example 5.12 exhibits almost all the conceptual elements that will lead Schenker to the final form of his analytical presentations. Furthermore, the notational devices of this example—the capped *Urlinie* tones, the separation of the sketches into distinct, vertically aligned levels, the slurs and dotted slurs used to group together the different linear progressions—did not change significantly during the remaining issues of *Tonwille* (1923 and 1924) or in the first two volumes of *Das Meisterwerk in der Musik* (1925 and 1926), although they did undergo much refinement in detail. The real progress made during these years in regard to the concept of the *Ursatz* was in Schenker's realization that the simple contrapuntal settings of *Urlinien* that he had begun to uncover were connected at the very deepest level to the fundamental principles of counterpoint he had set forth in *Counterpoint* some years earlier. It is in this realization that we discover the final stage in the growth of the *Ursatz* concept and, at the same time, the ultimate significance of the *Ursatz* as the prototype of all melody and harmony.

It is not possible to determine from the published writings precisely when Schenker began to see all *Ursätze* as sharing their basic characteristics, but it is clear that by 1925, in the first volume of *Meisterwerk*, he had generalized the specific conceptions embodied in example 5.12. "The task of the composer," he writes in that volume, "is composing out a chord; this task leads him from a background *Ursatz* through conceptual extensions [*Prolongationen*] and diminutions, to a foreground setting."[17] Furthermore, the analytical sketches in that volume reveal that the generalized conception of the *Ursatz* already carried with it the notions that the *Urlinie* consisted of a filling-in of the tonal space in a descent from the eighth, fifth, or third scale degrees to the first scale degree of the diatonic order, and that its counterpoint consisted of an arpeggiation from the first scale degree to the fifth and then back to the first, just as the particular case in example 5.12 had indicated. In addition, by saying that the music is the composing-out of a chord, Schenker indicated that he had now resolved even the basic and simple *Ursatz* into its primitive form—the vertical triad.

Having come this far in tracing the genesis of the *Ursatz*, we are at last in a position to explain what is perhaps most mysterious about it: why does Schenker ascribe *organic* characteristics to it?

The two voices of the *Ursatz* form what Schenker calls an *Aussensatz*— that is, a contrapuntal setting of outer voices—which he describes, in the first volume of *Meisterwerk*, as follows: "The *Aussensatz* in strict counterpoint is a two-voice setting fashioned from the highest and lowest voices; in free composition it is also the two-voice setting fashioned from the highest and lowest voices, but it actually functions in an extended sense as the setting of an upper and an inner voice above an imagined lower voice, which carries the fundamental tones of the scale degrees."[18] Example 5.13 shows an application of the *Aussensatz* concept to the simple *Ursatz* form that begins on the third scale degree of the diatonic order. At *a*, the lowest tone, in parentheses, stands for Schenker's "imagined lower voice"—in this case, the fundamental of the generative triad of which the *Ursatz* is the first elaboration. At *b*, consideration of the highest and lowest

Example 5.13. Genesis of the *Ursatz*

voices of *a* reveals the contrapuntal pattern of the dissonant passing tone, which first appears in strict counterpoint during the study of the second species in two voices. The three voices at *a*, on the other hand, present the model of the leaping passing tone, which first appears in strict counterpoint during the study of the second species in three voices.

In the second volume of *Counterpoint* (1922), Schenker pointed out the significance of the dissonant passing tone: in the systematic study of strict counterpoint, it is the first means of creating melodic extension:

> Alongside all of the corporality ... of the intervals available in strict counterpoint, the first appearance of the dissonant passing tone produces a curious intrusion of the imaginary: it consists in the covert retention, by the ear, of the consonant point of departure that accompanies the dissonant passing tone on its journey through the third-space. It is as though the dissonance would always carry with it the impression of its consonant origin. . . . The implications of this effect are of great importance: we recognize in the dissonant passing tone the most dependable—indeed the only—vehicle of melodic content.[19]

The dissonant passing tone, then, is the underlying model of all melodic motion, and the *Ursatz* embodies this universal melodic model in the relationship between the *Urlinie* and the fundamental tone of the imagined lower voice.

On the other hand, the motion presented by the bass arpeggiation of the *Ursatz* is also a contrapuntal model. In strict three-voice counterpoint, as shown at *c* in example 5.13, a dissonant passing tone in one voice can appropriate a consonant leap in another voice, creating the phenomenon Schenker called the "leaping passing tone." As he explains it, the inner voice in the example, even though it leaps, is just as much a passing motion as the upper voice because it participates in the unifying power of the dissonant passing tone.[20] When viewed in the context of the *Ursatz*, however, the leaping passing tone takes on the role of an archetype; for when the imagined lowest voice at *a* is removed—at it must be, since it is never present in the actual music—the combination of dissonant passing tone and leaping passing tone, shown at *d*, gives the impression of a new, independent verticality. The contrapuntal model of the leaping passing tone thus becomes the universal model for all harmonic generation in music.

The ultimate significance of the *Ursatz*, then, is that it functions as the archetype for all musical pitch relations because it encapsulates symbolically both the horizontal and the vertical aspects of pitch relations. It is at the same time the universal model of both melody and harmony. The *Ursatz* offers, in the most concise and fertile formula, all there is to know about the elaborational process that leads through the voice leading levels toward the musical surface. All transformations and metamorphoses of the

Ursatz operate according to principles already present in the prototype. It is for this reason that Schenker ascribes organic qualities to the *Ursatz*: like a seed or an egg, it holds within itself the principle and the pattern of its future growth.

Here the story of the growth of the *Ursatz* comes to an end; for it is this fully formed conception of the *Ursatz* as a generative archetype, present already in the first two volumes of *Meisterwerk*, that occupied Schenker's thought for the rest of his life. The great achievements that followed were not directed toward further development of the concept, but rather toward greater understanding of its properties. On the one hand, Schenker had to work out the consequences of the *Ursatz*, the possible ways in which such an archetypal kernel could promulgate itself through the levels; on the other hand, he had to devise a new and precise notation that could communicate those possibilities. The progress of the latter task can be judged by glancing at the analysis of the "Eroica" in the third volume of *Meisterwerk* (1930); since the notational devices used in this analysis are virtually identical with those used in the *Fünf Urlinie-Tafeln* (1932) and in *Free Composition*, a great deal of the work on notation was clearly completed during the publication hiatus between 1926 and 1930. As for the former task—the comprehensive account of possible *Ursatz* transformations—its completion is recorded in *Free Composition* itself, through which Schenker bequeathed the enigmatic *Ursatz* concept to a fascinated and sometimes perplexed posterity.

NOTES

1. Table 5.1 (p. 84) provides a chronology of Schenker's publications cited in this paper. Since the footnotes refer to translations whenever possible, the table also includes, for ease of reference, bibliographic information for all the original editions.
2. Heinrich Schenker, *Counterpoint*, trans. John Rothgeb and Jürgen Thym, ed. John Rothgeb (New York: Schirmer Books, 1987), vol. 1, pp. 94–95. William Rothstein has reminded me that Schenker's analysis of J. S. Bach's *Chromatic Fantasy and Fugue*, which was published a year before the first volume of *Counterpoint*, makes some use of the concept of melodic fluency. (Heinrich Schenker, *J. S. Bach's Chromatic Fantasy and Fugue: Critical Edition with Commentary,* trans. and ed. Hedi Siegel [New York: Schirmer Books, 1984].) This is very true; but since Schenker does not discuss the concept there, and since he himself views the concept as having been introduced in the first volume of *Counterpoint* (see note 10 below), I have elected to pass over the earlier work. In any case, Schenker's work on the *Fantasy and Fugue*

Table 5.1
Chronology of Schenker's Works Cited, 1909–1935

1909	*J. S. Bach: Chromatische Phantasie und Fuge*. Vienna: Universal Edition.
1910	*Kontrapunkt, erster Teil. Neue musikalische Theorien und Phantasien*, Vol. 2. Vienna: Universal Edition.
1912	*Beethoven neunte Sinfonie*. Vienna: Universal Edition.
1913	*Beethoven: Op. 109. Erläuterungs-Ausgaben der letzten fünf Sonaten Beethovens*. Vienna: Universal Edition.
1914	*Beethoven: Op. 110. Erläuterungs-Ausgaben der letzten fünf Sonaten Beethovens*. Vienna: Universal Edition.
1915	*Beethoven: Op. 111. Erläuterungs-Ausgaben der letzten fünf Sonaten Beethovens*. Vienna: Universal Edition.
1920	*Beethoven: Op. 101. Erläuterungs-Ausgaben der letzten fünf Sonaten Beethovens*. Vienna: Universal Edition.
1921	*Der Tonwille*, Vol. 1. Vienna: A. Gutmann Verlag.
1922	*Der Tonwille*, Vols. 2–3. Vienna: A. Gutmann Verlag. *Kontrapunkt, zweiter Teil. Neue musikalische Theorien und Phantasien*, Vol. 2. Vienna: Universal Edition.
1923	*Der Tonwille*, Vols. 4–6. Vienna: A. Gutmann Verlag.
1924	*Der Tonwille*, Vols. 7–10. Vienna: A. Gutmann Verlag.
1925	*Das Meisterwerk in der Musik*, Vol. 1. Munich: Drei Masken Verlag.
1926	*Das Meisterwerk in der Musik*, Vol. 2. Munich: Drei Masken Verlag.
1930	*Das Meisterwerk in der Musik*, Vol. 3. Munich: Drei Masken Verlag.
1932	*Fünf Urlinie-Tafeln*. Vienna: Universal Edition.
1935	*Der freie Satz. Neue Musikalische Theorien und Phantasien*, Vol. 3. Vienna: Universal Edition.

no doubt proceeded at the same time as work on *Counterpoint*, so that, for all practical purposes, the examples of melodic fluency in the former can be regarded as contemporaneous with the discussion in the latter.

3. Schenker, *Counterpoint*, 1:95.

4. Example 5.1 is from Schenker, *Counterpoint*, 1:96.

5. Example 5.2 is from Schenker, *Counterpoint*, 1:71.

6. Example 5.3 is from Schenker, *Beethoven: Op. 109*, p. 43; rev. ed., ed. Oswald Jonas (Vienna: Universal Edition, 1971), p. 43. Example 5.4 is from Schenker, *Beethoven: Op. 110*, p. 37; rev. ed., ed. Oswald Jonas (Vienna: Universal Edition, 1972), p. 32.

7. Examples 5.5 and 5.6 are from Schenker, *Beethoven: Op. 111*, p. 33; rev. ed., ed. Oswald Jonas (Vienna: Universal Edition, 1971), p. 8.

8. Example 5.7 is from Schenker, *Beethoven: Op. 110*, p. 38; rev. ed., p. 34.

9. The sketches of example 5.8 are from Schenker, *Beethoven: Op. 110*, pp. 47–48; rev. ed., pp. 54–56.

10. Schenker, *Beethoven: Op. 101,* p. 22; rev. ed., ed. Oswald Jonas (Vienna: Universal Edition, 1972), pp. 7–9.

11. Example 5.9 is from Schenker, *Beethoven: Op. 101*, p. 36; rev. ed., p. 35.

12. Example 5.10 is from Schenker, *Beethoven: Op. 101*, p. 44; rev. ed., pp. 52–53.

13. William Pastille, "Heinrich Schenker, Anti-Organicist," *19th-Century Music* 8 (1984): 34; Schenker, "Mozart: Sonate A-Moll," *Der Tonwille* 2 (1922): 7–24.

14. Example 5.11 is from Schenker, "J. S. Bach: Zwölf kleine Praeludien, Nr. 2," *Der Tonwille* 4 (1923): 7, and the inserted *Urlinie-Tafeln*.

15. Example 5.12 is from Schenker, "J. S. Bach: Zwölf kleine Praeludien, Nr. 5," *Der Tonwille* 5 (1923): 8.

16. Schenker, "Urlinie und Stimmfuhrung," *Der Tonwille* 5 (1923): 45.

17. Schenker, "Fortsetzung der Urlinie-Betrachtungen," in *Meisterwerk*, 1:188.

18. Ibid.

19. Schenker, *Counterpoint*, 2:57–58.

20. Schenker, *Counterpoint*, 2:181–182.

Rhythmic Displacement and Rhythmic Normalization

◆

William Rothstein

The interrelations between Schenker's theories and the rhythmic structure of tonal music have been explored by a number of authors since 1970.[1] In an earlier work (my Ph.D. dissertation), I showed that much profound thinking about rhythmic structure is already contained in Schenker's own analyses and, to a lesser degree, in his writings.[2] This essay is adapted from one chapter in that dissertation, entitled "Rhythmic Normalization"; I present here in as general a form as possible the conclusions drawn in that chapter. Whereas the dissertation as a whole represented primarily an exegesis of Schenker's thought, here I present my own ideas, which, however, are intimately related to Schenker's. Where an idea originates with Schenker, that fact is indicated.

To understand what the term *rhythmic normalization* means, one first needs to understand the better-known concept of *rhythmic displacement*. The most obvious form of rhythmic displacement is syncopation—that type of rhythm in which musical events occur on relatively weak parts of the bar and fail to occur on relatively strong parts. (By "musical events" I mean principally attacks.) Perhaps the simplest example of syncopation is provided by the fourth species of counterpoint as expounded by J. J. Fux (1725; example 6.1).

In the first part of example 6.1, the upper voice contains attacks only on the weaker of the two beats in each measure; hence it is syncopated. Fux relates this situation to that shown in the second part of the example, in which, after the first measure, attacks occur only on downbeats. In other words, he relates fourth-species counterpoint directly to first-species counterpoint. Specifically, he points out that example 6.1a (fourth species) transforms into example 6.1b (first species) "if the retardations [syncopations] are removed."[3]

When Fux speaks of retardations being "removed" from example 6.1a,

Example 6.1. Fux, *Gradus ad Parnassum*, fourth- and first-species progressions

he implies that they were "added" to something in the first place—obviously, to the first-species progression in example 6.1b. In terms of this study, example 6.1b represents the *normal* version of the contrapuntal passage, example 6.1a the *displaced* version. (The first measure is the same in both versions, though Fux might well have shifted the upper voice's G back to the initial downbeat in example 6.1b.) Given example 6.1a, example 6.1b is its *normalization*. Given example 6.1b, example 6.1a is one possible *displacement* of it (there are others).[4] The relationship between the two concepts is reciprocal, though not one to one.

The extreme simplicity of this little example should not blind us to the wealth of relational implications opened up by the concepts involved, nor to the perceptual implications. For if a musical passage can be rhythmically normalized, there arises at least the possibility of hearing the given, displaced version *in terms of* its normalization—or, more precisely, hearing it as a *transformation* of that normalization—even if the latter is not literally present anywhere in the music. The normalization, in other words, may be inferred from the given passage, which is then understood as a displaced version of it.[5]

The advantage of such an understanding is this: it allows the listener to perceive the given, displaced version of a musical passage as embodying a certain rhythmic tension, which can be measured—both qualitatively and quantitatively—against the relatively less tense normal version. (The measurement is quantitative in that it specifies the number of beats by which any tone has been displaced.) Rhythmic displacement yields an increase in subjectively felt tension; normalization removes the tension and, in so doing, identifies its origin. From this viewpoint, the purpose of rhythmic normalization is to describe the source, quality, and amount of rhythmic tension contained in a given passage. *Mutatis mutandis*, this is a function that Schenkerian reduction serves in the domain of tonal structure.

To be complete, our account of rhythmic normalization would have to include the normalization of phrase lengths, a subject that has been explored, from a Schenkerian point of view, by Carl Schachter, Charles Burkhart, and the present author.[6] Space does not permit such a full account here. However, the similarity that we have already noted between the tonal and rhythmic domains extends to the domain of phrase lengths as well. In this last domain, a normal underlying form—most often a phrase of four or eight measures—may be transformed by expansion or contraction, or by any of several other manipulations.[7] In this as in the other domains, the coexistence of normal and transformed versions of the same passage results in a hierarchical structure in which the normal version is always conceptually prior to its transformations.

Furthermore, in each domain the structural hierarchy corresponds to specific kinds of musical tension and resolution (or relaxation). In fact, specifying the structural hierarchy is probably the best way (because it is the most precise) to describe musical tension and relaxation.[8] Instead of resorting immediately to hermeneutic interpretations (which may still be valuable as part of a more comprehensive critical act), the analyst can demonstrate the source, quality, and amount of musical tension directly, *in tones*. This is possible, however, only if it is understood by analyst and reader alike that hierarchical structure and musical affect stand in the most intimate relation to each other.

The general situation may be stated as follows. In tonal music we continually hear the specific, the distinctive, and the surprising in relation to the general, the normal, and the expected; the abnormal is understood in terms of the normal. Tension is understood to arise from the difference between the given musical phenomena (which, in a piece of any artistic interest, are bound to contain surprises and abnormalities) and the musical norms from which those phenomena depart. The distance between the musical surface and the underlying norms fluctuates within a composition, yielding for the listener a corresponding fluctuation of tension. It is usual in tonal music for the distance between surface and norm, and thus the level of tension, to be relatively small at cadences, and especially at the structural close of a composition (either the final cadence or the cadence that closes the fundamental structure). The distance between surface and norm is generally greater elsewhere; the point of greatest distance, and thus of maximum tension, is what most listeners will intuitively regard as the climax of a passage or a piece.[9]

Simple Normalizations

The relationship between rhythmic normalization and Schenkerian reduction is very close, indeed even closer than has been suggested thus far. It has been a crucial contribution of Schenkerian theory that rhythmic structure depends enormously on pitch structure; this is as true of rhythmic normalization as it is of other aspects of rhythm (for example, the kinds of rhythmic stratification first discussed by Maury Yeston).[10] The pitch structures on which normalization depends are precisely those hierarchical structures embodied by the structural levels of Schenkerian theory.

Example 6.2 shows three simple instances of rhythmic normalization. Unlike example 6.1, none of these examples would be permitted in species counterpoint according to Fux or Schenker. The "forbidden" aspect, in each case, is the metrical position of the dissonance, which in species counterpoint may appear on the downbeat only as a suspension in fourth and fifth species.

Example 6.2a shows a dissonant appoggiatura resolving to a consonance. Since an appoggiatura may be regarded as an unprepared suspension, its normalization is similar to that of a suspension (compare example 6.1). Thus, the dissonance is understood to delay the appearance of the consonance, which "rightly" belongs on the downbeat. The *underlying duration* of the consonance—that is, the duration of the consonant interval in the normalized version—is a full measure.

Example 6.2b shows an accented upper neighbor resolving back to the original consonance without a change of harmony. Normalization here takes place in two stages. First, the accented metrical position of the neighbor note is understood to arise from a rhythmic shift—that is, from the displacement of a more normal, unaccented neighbor.[11] In the second stage, the entire example is reduced to the original consonance, the underlying duration of which is understood to be two measures. (Actually, the first stage of normalization in example 6.2b could be eliminated by treating the accented neighbor note exactly like the appoggiatura in example 6.2a; one would thus arrive at the single consonance [E over C] in one step instead of two.)

Example 6.2c shows an accented passing tone within the space of a third, E–G. As in example 6.2b, the harmony does not change; a C-major

Example 6.2. Rhythmic normalizations

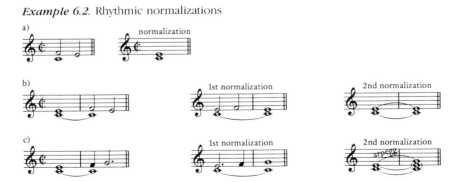

triad is the implicit harmonic background. Here, too, normalization proceeds in two stages. In the first stage, the accented passing tone F is understood to result from the displacement of a regular, unaccented passing tone. Then, in the "second normalization," the passing tone is reduced out, leaving an arpeggiated third in an equal rhythm of whole notes. (The durational inequality of F and G is addressed below.) Because of the continuing C-major harmony, E is understood to remain in effect while G is sounding; this implied continuation is indicated by the parentheses around E in the second measure.[12]

It should be noted that our results in example 6.2 are exactly what would have resulted from conventional Schenkerian reduction except that, in our analyses, the durations of all tones are specified at every level.

The harmonic aspect of example 6.2 is significant. In each of the three cases, a single harmony underlies the entire example; each time, at least one of the melodic tones involved has an underlying duration equal to that of the harmony as a whole. As we shall see, the underlying duration of melodic tones is closely linked to the durations of harmonies. By the same token, the rhythm of a succession of melodic tones in a normalized passage depends on that passage's harmonic rhythm.

Although it would be tedious to demonstrate the point in detail, the conclusions we derived from example 6.2 would apply equally well to vertical combinations of accented dissonances—that is, to accented linear chords (appoggiatura chords, suspension chords, accented passing and neighboring chords). With unaccented linear chords, normalization occurs automatically when we "reduce out" those chords; this is the same procedure that we followed with the unaccented dissonant notes in the parts of examples 6.2b and 6.2c labeled "first normalization."

In example 6.2c, I have purposely made the rhythm of the dissonance and its resolution unequal, with a shorter dissonance (F) and a longer resolution (G). As Peter Westergaard points out in his book *An Introduction to Tonal Theory*, this is an abnormal way to subdivide a metrical unit (in this case the second measure of the example).[13] Any metrical unit is normally subdivided either into equal values—for example, equal half notes, quarter notes, or eighth notes—or into unequal values with the longest value occurring first—for example, a dotted half note followed by a quarter note. In species counterpoint, the same norm is expressed by the rules governing the combination of note values in fifth species.[14] This norm is independent of pitch relationships. Using terms introduced by Carl Schachter, it is a norm of durational rhythm rather than of tonal rhythm.[15]

Also belonging to the realm of durational rhythm is a phenomenon that I term *equalization*. A series of equal note values has a tendency to perpetuate itself by a sort of rhythmic inertia; this is true not only in the late Baroque (where the tendency is certainly strongest) but in later tonal music as well. In a polyphonic texture, the maintenance of equal values in any voice or voices often leads to contrapuntal clashes that probably would have been avoided otherwise. Such is frequently the origin of what Schenker called deceptive or "inauthentic" intervals (*uneigentliche Intervalle*).[16] Schenker himself was aware of equalization: in *Free Composition* he ascribes one example of a deceptive interval to "an equalizing into eighths" because of "the necessity of avoiding the direct juxtaposition of different rhythmic values."[17]

The Rule of Simultaneity and the Rule of Arpeggiation

Two other norms invoked in examples 6.1 and 6.2 involve pitch relationships and thus fall at least partly into Schachter's category of tonal rhythm. First, it is normal for a dissonance to appear in a less accented metrical position than its resolution, abnormal for it to appear in a more accented position. (This norm was explicitly invoked in examples 6.2b and 6.2c.) Second, it is normal, in a two-voice texture, for harmonic intervals (that is, intervals involving both voices and belonging to the underlying triad or seventh chord) to be struck together; it is abnormal for such intervals to appear in staggered form as they do in examples 6.1 and 6.2a.[18] This latter norm is of great importance to the theory and practice of rhythmic normalization; henceforth I will call it the *rule of simultaneity*.

In the "second normalization" of example 6.2c, C and E are struck together; G, which also belongs to the underlying C-major triad, arrives only later. The example thus constitutes an arpeggiation. The rule of simultaneity applies to three-note (and larger) arpeggiations exactly as it does to single harmonic intervals; hence we may speak of a *rule of arpeggiation*, according to which all tones of an arpeggiated harmony "belong" together as a vertical chord. In a normalized version, the tones of an arpeggiation will eventually be realigned so that the displaced arpeggiation tones are restored to the vertical chord from which they originate. I say "eventually" because the verticalization may not occur until a relatively late stage of normalization. In example 6.2c, for instance, the final stage of normalization—the stage following the last one shown in the example itself—would contain a two-measure-long C-major triad with G in the soprano (example 6.3).

As stated, the rule of arpeggiation specifies only that the tones of an arpeggiation will appear simultaneously, as a chord, at some level of structure nearer the background. What remains to be specified is (1) the rhythmic point at which the simultaneity takes effect and (2) its underlying duration. The latter is determined by the former; that is, the underlying duration of any harmony (except the last one in a piece) is equal to the

Example 6.3. Final normalization

temporal distance between the initiation point of that harmony and the initiation point of the following harmony.

Harmonic initiation points, in the foreground, are usually readily apparent from the musical surface. (More complexities arise where middleground harmonies are involved.) Where such initiation points are not obvious, other contextual factors may be decisive. Regarding those factors, a few principles seem to apply fairly generally. If harmonies have been changing at an even rate (for example, one harmony per bar), the listener will tend to perceive that rate as maintained unless some change is clearly signaled. Thus, if there is any ambiguity in the harmonic rhythm, it will tend to be resolved in favor of the prevailing harmonic rhythm wherever possible.

A second principle is that harmonies tend to begin on relatively strong beats rather than on relatively weak ones. When a harmony begins on a weak beat and is continued into the next stronger beat, a harmonic syncopation results. As the term implies, such a syncopation will tend to be heard as a displacement of the normal harmonic rhythm, especially if other harmonic changes occur on relatively strong beats.[19] Thus a harmonic syncopation can itself be normalized; an instance of such normalization (from Schumann's op. 12, no. 8) is shown in example 6.4. When a harmonic syncopation is normalized, the *underlying initiation point* of the harmony will not be the same as its *surface initiation point*. The difference between the two initiation points is a measure of the rhythmic tension created by the displacement.

Example 6.4. Schumann, "Ende vom Lied" (op. 12, no. 8), bars 21–27 and reduction

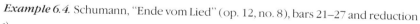

The rule of arpeggiation implies that, in any kind of arpeggiated texture, all tones belonging to the same harmony may be understood to derive from a vertical chord that has a certain underlying duration. This conclusion corresponds to musical experience. For example, a strummed accompaniment or an Alberti bass figuration is heard as a rhythmic activation of a series of chords, and thus a transformation of a chordal texture.

Arpeggiated textures are especially useful to composers where parallel fifths and octaves threaten. It is well known that, under certain conditions, arpeggiated figurations can break up parallel fifths and octaves to a point that the parallels become unobjectionable. Certain other types of figuration, especially suspensions and other accented dissonances, can serve a similar function.[20] In fact, avoiding faulty parallels is often the reason for a rhythmic displacement. When such displacements are normalized, the underlying parallels will naturally come to the fore. This is not a problem; what is important is to understand the relationship between the underlying progression and the musical surface, including the role that the displacement plays in rendering the parallels harmless. As Schenker writes in *Free Composition*, "The middleground frequently displays forbidden successions; it is then the task of the foreground to eliminate them." And further, "The foreground may contain 8–8 or 5–5 successions that would have to be considered faulty were their removal not achieved locally by foreground devices."[21]

The implications of the rule of arpeggiation go far beyond such obvious cases as Alberti basses. For example, a polyphonic or compound melody (a phenomenon heavily dependent on arpeggiation) is subject to the same rule. A polyphonic melody will reduce to a chordal texture when its non-chord tones are reduced out, its constituent voices are verticalized, and the rule of arpeggiation is applied. I like to think of this latent chordal texture as a sort of imaginary continuo accompaniment that underlies every piece of tonal music—regardless of scoring, texture, or date of composition.[22]

Example 6.5 illustrates both the rule of arpeggiation and the imaginary continuo. It is taken from Robert Schumann's arrangement, for violin and piano, of J. S. Bach's Sonatas and Partitas for unaccompanied violin.

Schenker wrote that in these arrangements "the piano part does not constitute an obbligato to the violin part, nor does it limit itself to a more or less free realization of an imagined figured bass."[23] In example 6.5, however, the piano part resembles nothing so much as "[the] more or less free realization of an imagined figured bass." Like most continuo parts, this one clarifies the voice leading of the music it accompanies. For example, the origin of d^1 in the first measure from an implied $c^{\sharp 1}$ is made clear by the doubling of both tones an octave higher in the piano.[24] The origin of $g^{\sharp}$ in the second bar from an implied $f^{\sharp}$ (which, of course, cannot

Example 6.5. Bach-Schumann, Courante (from B-minor Partita), bars 33–37

be played on the violin as normally tuned) is clarified by the piano's statement of those tones in the same register. On the downbeat of the fourth bar Schumann adds the tone $c^{\sharp 1}$, which is implied by the presence of e^2 in the violin; the progression of parallel tenths in bars 3–5 is thus maintained, as it is by Schumann's placement of g^2 on the downbeat of bar 5. Only Schumann's bass line in bars 1–3 goes a little beyond the definite implications of Bach's voice leading; here Schumann adds a descending fifth-progression, $f^{\sharp}$–B, to the voices already present in the violin.[25]

Schumann's verticalizations in example 6.5 are mostly obvious; they are straightforward applications of the rule of arpeggiation. A detail of rhythm in the first bar, however, deserves comment. The violin's first five eighth notes in that bar form an $F^{\sharp}$-major harmony. But with the entrance of d^1 on the last eighth, the listener is led to reevaluate the local chordal membership of the immediately preceding $f^{\sharp 1}$. What the listener is responding to here is the prevailing harmonic rhythm of the piece, which discourages hearing a change of chord on the weak half of any beat. Accordingly, the change to a B-minor sonority—a $^6_3$ chord, in Schumann's setting—is heard to occur on the third beat of the measure, not on the last eighth note. (From a larger point of view, however, there is no change of harmony in bar 1; V of B minor remains in effect until bar 3. A change of chord occurs only in the most local sense, which is the sense that a continuo accompanist would be dealing with if Bach had supplied an actual figured bass.)

It follows, therefore, that in the underlying voice leading of bar 1, the motions from $a^{\sharp 1}$ to b^1, and from the implied $c^{\sharp 1}$ to d^1, occur precisely on the third beat. This is true not only in Schumann's setting of the piece, but—more important—in Bach's. The imaginary continuo, here realized by another composer of genius, expresses the web of chords and voice leading that underlies Bach's texture.

At higher structural levels, applying the rule of arpeggiation is often less straightforward then it is at the chord-to-chord level that has been our focus thus far. In figure 40 of *Free Composition*, for instance, Schenker presents a series of middleground graphs showing initial arpeggiations to the primary tone of a fundamental line. In every example shown, the harmony outlined by arpeggiation is the tonic. In several examples, however, the primary tone, which forms the peak of the arpeggiation, arrives over a non-tonic harmony: III♯ in examples 1 and 10 (Chopin's "Military" Polonaise and "Harp" Etude), IV⁷ in example 6 (the slow movement of Beethoven's "Funeral March" Sonata), and a cadential ⁶₄ in example 7 (Chopin's Mazurka in A♭ major, op. 24, no. 3). In each of these examples (all, incidentally, involving 3̂ as primary tone), the rule of arpeggiation stipulates that the tones of the initial tonic arpeggiation belong together as a vertical chord starting at the beginning of the piece. Since each piece begins with a tonic harmony in the middleground (the Chopin mazurka begins with an auxiliary V in the foreground), the later tones of the initial arpeggiation may be understood as having been delayed from that harmonic initiation point. Therefore, in a normalized version, the primary tone would appear directly over the initial tonic harmony. The first interval of the fundamental structure—primary tone in the soprano, tonic note in the bass—would thus appear as a simultaneity.[26]

Arpeggiations occurring in the bass must be counted as a special class, corresponding to the unique function of the bass voice in general. It is necessary to distinguish two types of bass arpeggiation: (1) the arpeggiation that unfolds a single harmony; (2) the arpeggiation that connects two different harmonies. The first type is similar to arpeggiations in other voices, and the rule of arpeggiation applies to it in full force. The second type, which I call the *connective bass arpeggiation*, differs from other arpeggiations; the rule of arpeggiation applies to it only in a very limited way.

If a bass arpeggiation unfolds a single harmony, this does not necessarily mean that one root is maintained through every chord of the passage. There may be local root changes, but the arpeggiation *as a whole* prolongs a single root. For example, the progression I–III–V–I prolongs the tonic harmony through arpeggiation; in a Schenkerian reduction, only the I harmony would appear at a higher structural level. Rhythmically speaking, the tonic harmony, with its root in the bass, has an underlying duration equal to the actual duration of the entire arpeggiation. In this case, tonal reduction and rhythmic normalization are nearly identical operations, because no rhythmic displacement is involved. Normalization merely specifies the underlying duration of the prolonged tonic harmony (this is something that tonal reduction does only by implication).

A very different case is presented by the common harmonic progression I–VI–IV, which is usually found in the context of the complete cadential progression I–VI–IV–V–I. The first three of these chords are commonly said to form an arpeggiation because the three bass tones involved outline a triad, namely, IV. But I–VI–IV in this context does not *prolong* IV; when the progression is reduced, the I and VI triads do not disappear in favor of the subdominant. Rather, VI is a dividing point within the more basic motion from I to IV, while the IV itself is a harmonic prefix to V (as is expressed by the terms "pre-dominant" and "dominant prep-aration"). Underlying the complete progression is I–V–I, a true arpeggia-tion prolonging the tonic. By contrast, if the so-called arpeggiation I–VI–IV is taken literally, the rule of arpeggiation stipulates that only the IV harmony would appear at some higher level; furthermore, the IV har-mony's underlying initiation point would be placed at the beginning of the progression, where the musical surface shows the tonic! This analytical result contradicts the prolongational structure of the progression so fun-damentally that we must do one of two things: either discard the rule of arpeggiation as having been disproved, or recognize this particular pro-gression as something other than an arpeggiation.

The second course is the more satisfactory. I–VI–IV is not a true arpeggiation but a connective motion emphasizing common tones: the root of VI (the intermediate triad) anticipates the third of IV (the immediate goal), while the tonic pitch class is common to all three triads.[27] The prolongational structure, which is largely independent of rhythm, deter-mines this outcome. Rhythmic analysis of the progression ought to follow the prolongational structure at every stage: I–VI–IV–V–I reduces first to I–IV–V–I, then to I–V–I, and finally to the tonic triad itself. The underlying initiation point of each harmony is the same as its surface initiation point so long as that harmony is still present in the reduction. (However, local syncopations or other small-scale rhythmic disturbances [such as antici-pations] may displace the surface initiation point of any harmony.)

The most common ascending bass arpeggiation is I–III–V; this may also appear as I–I⁶–V. If a tonic does not follow the V, V generally functions either as a point of interruption (in which case the I arrives eventually) or as an applied divider (also known as a "back-relating dominant").[28] An applied divider prolongs the harmony to which it is applied—in this case, the tonic. Since the tonic harmony is precisely what the arpeggiation outlines in the bass, there is no conflict between the bass arpeggiation and the harmonic prolongation; hence the rule of arpeggiation applies without difficulty. The underlying initiation point of the tonic is the same as its surface initiation point, absent any local syncopation or anticipation.

There are some descending bass arpeggiations in which the harmon-ies' underlying initiation points and underlying durations are dependent not only on the prolongational structure but also on other, contextual factors. For example, in an auxiliary progression V–I (which outlines the fifth and root of the tonic triad), the V will be heard to delay the I—and thus the initiation point of the tonic will be heard as displaced—if the V

Example 6.6. Schenker, *Free Composition*, fig. 110, a1 and a2

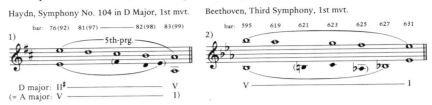

is metrically accented relative to the I.[29] If this is not the case, the V might be heard as an upbeat to the I on either a small or a large metrical level; as Carl Schachter has pointed out, the opening of Chopin's "Revolutionary" Etude is an example of a large-scale upbeat V^7–I.[30] Where V acts as an upbeat to I, the prevailing harmonic rhythm usually discourages placing the underlying initiation point of the tonic on the upbeat.

Yet another type of V–I situation is the auxiliary cadence V–I in the middle of a piece, often in a secondary (that is, non-tonic) key. Example 6.6, from *Free Composition*, shows two instances of this, one in a secondary key and one in the main key. As Schenker noted of auxiliary cadences in general, "Despite the degrees which belong to the forthcoming root, the space up to its actual entrance belongs conceptually to the preceding harmony." In other words, the underlying initiation point of the (local) tonic is not displaced when an auxiliary cadence occurs in the middle of a piece; in principle, the surface and underlying initiation points of the (local) tonic are identical (absent any local syncopation, etc.).[31]

Linear Progressions and the Rule of the Primary Tone

In Schenkerian theory, a linear progression (*Zug*) is always the composing-out of a specific chordal interval belonging either to a triad or a seventh chord.[32] Despite its stepwise appearance, therefore, a linear progression is in essence an arpeggiation filled in by passing tones. Given this fact, it seems only logical to extend the rule of arpeggiation a step further to account for filled as well as unfilled arpeggiations.

The principal chord tones in a linear progression are always two: the initial tone and the goal tone. Nevertheless, a linear progression may outline a two-, three-, or four-note arpeggiation. In a third-progression, the first and last tones form a two-note arpeggiation consisting of adjacent chord tones, such as the root and third, or third and fifth, of a triad. Fourth-progressions outline the space from the fifth of a triad up to its root, or from the root down to the fifth. Fifth-progressions outline three-note arpeggiations, because the first and last tones of the progression enclose one other chord tone between them. (The degree to which the middle chord tone is articulated, however, varies greatly; it may even appear as a dissonance in the foreground.) Sixth-progressions are similar, although there may be two intermediate chord tones if an inverted seventh chord is being arpeggiated. A seventh-progression connecting the root and seventh of a seventh chord arpeggiates the entire four-note chord. Octave-progressions usually outline a four-note triadic arpeggiation while also executing a change of register, either ascending or descending, of a single tone.

A linear progression *prolongs* the triad or seventh chord outlined by its arpeggiation tones. (Schenker speaks already in *Harmony* of the horizontalization of triads.)[33] If this melodic prolongation alone were taken into account, the rule of arpeggiation would require that the underlying initiation point of the arpeggiated chord be placed at the beginning of the linear progression, where the arpeggiating motion itself begins. As long as the accompanying voices fully support the prolongation of the arpeggiated chord, this analysis will be correct: for example, if a fifth-progression $\hat{5}$–$\hat{4}$–$\hat{3}$–$\hat{2}$–$\hat{1}$, prolonging I, is accompanied by a cadential harmonic progression beginning and ending with I, there is no conflict between melodic and harmonic prolongations, and thus no conflict regarding the underlying initiation point of the tonic harmony (which occurs beneath the $\hat{5}$ in this case). But if the accompanying voices somehow indicate that the chord being arpeggiated in the melody actually arrives, harmonically, only at the *end* of the linear progression (in our case, beneath the $\hat{1}$), a conflict exists: the melody begins arpeggiating its chord before the accompanying voices have arrived at it. Precisely this occurs if our descending fifth-progression is accompanied by an auxiliary cadence—for example, V–I or III–V–I (example 6.6).[34] In such cases, the bass and other accompanying voices take precedence over the melody in determining the underlying initiation point of the goal harmony, according to Schenker's principle regarding auxiliary cadences (see the quotation on p. 98). If the goal harmony arrives only at the end of the linear progression, the melodic line must be considered an anticipation of that harmony. This conflict between melodic and harmonic prolongations is a particularly subtle form of rhythmic displacement.

The underlying initiation point of each tone in an arpeggiation is the same as that of the harmony being arpeggiated. Hence any chord tones appearing *before* that point are to be understood as anticipations of the harmony (unless they are held in common with the preceding harmony). Any chord tones appearing *after* that point are to be understood as having been delayed from the underlying initiation point. This fact has special significance for linear progressions of the upper voice, a significance that Schenker points out in *Das Meisterwerk in der Musik*:

> Linear progressions of the upper voice, when descending, signify a motion into an inner voice of the same or the following chord; when ascending, they signify a motion from an inner voice to the upper voice.

The mentally retained initiating tone of a descending linear progression thus maintains the actual registral position of the upper voice [while the progression moves into an inner voice]; the mentally retained initiating tone of an ascending linear progression becomes an inner-voice tone.[35] [example 6.7]

Schenker's example shows, more clearly than his words, that the highest tone in each linear progression—the only tone that he considers truly to constitute the upper voice—is "mentally retained" throughout the progression. (Note that, in the examples involving a change of harmony, the "mentally retained" tone is common to both harmonies.) In our terms, the underlying duration of the upper-voice tone is equal to the literal duration of the entire progression. I call this principle the *rule of the primary tone*, though it is really a corollary to the rule of arpeggiation.

For the descending linear progressions in example 6.7a, the rule of the primary tone is virtually self-evident; it follows immediately from Schenker's principle of *das Festhalten des Kopftons* (the retention of the primary tone).[36] For the ascending linear progressions in example 6.7b, where the primary tone appears only at the end of the progression, the appeal of the rule to one's musical intuitions is less immediate. Example 6.7b shows that the primary tone is foreseen, as it were, from the beginning; it "belongs" with the initial bass tone as a simultaneous outer-voice interval (in example 6.7b, either a tenth c^1–e^2 or a twelfth c^1–g^2). The actual appearance of the primary tone at the end of the linear progression thus represents, according to Schenker, a rhythmic displacement of this conceptually prior interval.

Where ascending linear progressions are concerned, as in example 6.7b, the perceptual meaning of the rule of the primary tone varies according to the surrounding context. If the ascending progression occurs in the middle of a piece, so that the primary tone connects linearly with previous upper-voice tones, the linear progression is what Schenker calls a motion from an inner voice (*Untergreifszug*). In such cases the perception of a rhythmic delay of the primary tone is often strong, especially if previous linear progressions have *descended* from their respective primary tones. (The feeling of delay is especially prominent if the initiating tone of the ascent is metrically strong and the primary tone is metrically weak.) If the ascending progression begins the piece, it is an initial ascent or

Example 6.7. Schenker, *Das Meisterwerk in der Musik*, vol. 2

Anstieg, although, strictly speaking, Schenker's concept of the *Anstieg* belongs only to the first level of the middleground, not to later levels.[37] In the case of an initial ascent, the perception of rhythmic displacement can only be retrospective (this is equally true of initial arpeggiations). In example 6.7b, assuming that the ascending progressions shown are initial ascents, the literally presented opening interval (an octave) is actually more stable than the conceptually prior outer-voice interval (a tenth or twelfth). Only the subsequent content can determine unequivocally that c^2 belongs to an inner voice and that the true soprano tone is either e^2 (in the first example) or g^2 (in the second example). Once this is known, however, the listener can reinterpret the initial ascent as a gradual opening-up of the registral space between the structural bass and the structural soprano, relegating the ascent itself to inner-voice status. The structural soprano tone—the primary tone of the piece's fundamental line—can then be restored, in retrospect, to its "rightful" rhythmic position, which is the initiation point of the opening tonic harmony.

Linear progressions in inner voices are affected by the rule of arpeggiation, but the rule of the primary tone has less relevance for them. This is because the very concept of "primary tone" belongs to the upper voice. However, if there is a clear distinction between the structural value of two inner voices that are connected by a linear progression, the tone belonging to the voice of greater value may be considered the primary tone of the progression. In tonal music, some inner voices are obbligato voices, present throughout much or all of a composition, while others represent filling tones that come and go freely; the difference is chiefly one of continuity. If a linear progression connects a filling tone with an obbligato inner voice, the tone belonging to the obbligato voice is the primary tone of the progression, and the rule of the primary tone may be said to apply to it.[38]

Linear progressions of the lowest voice present a more complicated picture, just as bass arpeggiations do. However, the principles involved are the same as for bass arpeggiations; therefore, little needs to be added to our earlier discussion. Reduction of the linear progression to an arpeggiation and application of the principles governing bass arpeggiations will give the correct analytical result.

More on the Rule of Simultaneity

As the reader has probably noticed by now, the various manifestations of the rule of simultaneity—particularly the rule of arpeggiation and the rule of the primary tone—lead to a uniformly chordal texture once all rhythmic displacements in a passage have been normalized. This texture is essentially the "imaginary continuo" I spoke of earlier. The imaginary continuo is not restricted to four or five or even six voices; the number of voices may range freely from three upward. (Three is the minimum because, in tonal music, triads are implicit even in textures that apparently consist of only one or two voices.)

If, level by level, one reduces the tonal contents and normalizes the rhythmic position of all tones in a piece, one will gradually increase the total number of voices. This is because each apparently single-voiced motion (such as a linear progression) will ultimately reduce to a two-, three-, or four-note chord. Eventually, one might easily arrive at the result that the number of voices in a texture, at some underlying level, equals the total number of potential chord tones that exist between a given bass and a given soprano tone. Between great C and e^2, for example, there are 11 potential "voices" in a C-major chord if the outer tones are included in the count. If this C-major chord is composed out through arpeggiations and linear progressions, all 11 chord tones might easily be sounded—yielding, apparently, an 11-voiced chord in the background.

But such a clogging of the textural arteries is not a very revealing analytical exercise; nor does it reflect the true nature of tonal texture. The distinction cited earlier between obbligato inner voices and mere filler tones is crucial to an understanding of texture at underlying levels of structure. As one moves from the foreground toward the background, an obbligato voice at one level may become filler at the next level. As the background is approached, the outer voices always remain as structural anchors, but the inner voices increasingly become chordal filler, relegated from the obbligato texture to the imaginary continuo. Just as Baroque composers omitted writing out the filler voices belonging to the (actual) continuo, Schenkerian analysts should not grant filler voices of the imaginary continuo the same status as obbligato voices.

Thus, as the background is approached in a Schenkerian analysis, the number of voices is successively *reduced*, not enlarged. Eventually, the rule of simultaneity ensures that something like a first-species counterpoint will emerge; actually, given the presence of unsupported stretches in the fundamental line, what appears often looks like a loose mixture of first and second species. It is from this viewpoint that one can best appreciate Schenker's discussion, in *Free Composition*, of the relationship between species counterpoint and the first level of the middleground, including his much-quoted remarks on the contrapuntal origin of musical rhythm.[39] Schenker approaches his discussion synthetically, from the background forward; the approach used here is analytical, proceeding from the musical surface toward the background.

Analytical Application

Our discussion up to now has been mostly abstract. To remedy this situation, analyses of two brief passages are offered below. The passages, by Mozart and Chopin, are similar in several ways: both are for piano solo;

both are thematic statements occurring at the beginnings of their respective pieces; and both are exactly eight measures long. The last similarity reflects a deliberate decision: neither excerpt involves any expansion or other transformation of phrase lengths; nor is there any overlapping of phrases.[40] The phrase rhythm of the two examples has been kept deliberately simple so that our focus may be entirely on the issue at hand, namely, the rhythmic *position* of notes and harmonies.

The obvious similarities between the two passages conceal at least one important difference. The two excerpts exhibit markedly different textures, and the difference is one not merely of degree but of kind. In addition to its usual function of specifying rhythmic tensions and relaxations, rhythmic normalization here illuminates two different conceptions of writing for the piano.

Example 6.8 shows six levels of reduction from the initial statement of the rondo theme in the last movement of Mozart's Piano Sonata in B♭ Major, K. 333, starting from a level just below the surface of the music (level *a*) and ending with a stationary tonic triad (level *f*). Unlike a Schenkerian voice-leading graph, each level is notated in precise rhythmic values; levels *e* and *f* reduce the note values of the score by a factor of four.[41] Where the rhythmic position of any note differs from its position in the score, or from its position at some level nearer the surface, the difference represents a rhythmic normalization. Levels near the surface show rhythmic positions close to those of the score; deeper levels represent normalized rhythmic positions.[42]

Level *a* requires little comment. The interplay between the soprano and what might be called the first tenor (that is, the upper notes of the left hand) is highlighted; this consists of a tossing back and forth of the tones F and G. An implied suspension is revealed in the alto in bar 2. Several other implied tones (and implied continuations of sounded tones) are indicated by means of parentheses. Voice-leading connections are shown, but rather inefficiently; as Carl Schachter has noted, rhythmic reductions simply do not show voice leading as well as do conventional Schenkerian graphs.[43]

Following the rule of arpeggiation, level *b* verticalizes those chord tones that were still separated at level *a*. Level *b* also shows something that was implied in level *a*: the first tenor's g^1 in bar 1 is an anticipation. When the position of this note is normalized, parallel fifths are revealed between the I and II triads. The anticipation helps to conceal these underlying fifths at the surface; so, of course, does the fact that the preceding f^1 is implied rather than actually sounded.

In bar 3, level *b* shows that the principal bass tone in the first three-quarters of the bar is d^1 and not b♭. (This interpretation is confirmed by the bass line of bar 7.) The consequent doubling of D between the outer

Example 6.8. Mozart, K. 333, III, reductions of bars 1–8

voices helps to explain Mozart's diminution (level *a*), which avoids this doubling at the surface through a voice exchange. The same diminution also prevents any impression of parallel octaves ($E^\flat$–D) from arising in bars 2–3.

Finally, level *b* shows the connection between f^2 of bar 1 and the appoggiatura f^2 (really a long-range suspension) in bar 4. This connection, which amounts to a prolongation of f^2, explains the long duration given this tone at deeper levels of the analysis.

Level *c* illustrates the prolongation of the opening tonic harmony. It also shows, in bar 2, the doubled $E^\flat$ that Mozart carefully avoids at the musical surface. The II harmony of that measure (levels *a* and *b*) is revealed as a combined appoggiatura/suspension chord (with the embellishing notes in alto and first tenor) to the passing V.

So far, the texture in each four-measure phrase has comprised five obbligato voices at the start, thinning to four voices in the third measure of each phrase. This texture is maintained at level *d*. At this level, the inverted texture of bars 7–8, relative to bars 3–4, is altered so that the descending fifth-progression from F to $B^\flat$ is shown in the soprano rather than the first tenor. The principal melodic descents in both phrases thus correspond to each other rhythmically, even though they actually occur in different voices.

Level *d* is the last level to show the interrupted fifth-progression ($\hat{5}$–$\hat{2}$ ‖ $\hat{5}$–$\hat{1}$). At level *e*, which is also the first durational reduction, the cadential $^6_4$ chords of bars 4 and 7 are reduced to plain dominant triads, thus eliminating $\hat{3}$ from each descent. The II harmonies of bars 3 and 7 are also reduced out, since their bass note $e^\flat$ is an incomplete lower neighbor to f (the V) and the soprano note $\hat{4}$ is, like $\hat{3}$, a passing tone between $\hat{5}$ and $\hat{2}$. The primary tone f^2 is thus shown as sustained throughout the entire eight-measure period. What linear motion remains is an interrupted *third-progression* in an inner voice (here shown as the alto). At some remote level of reduction, most $\hat{5}$–$\hat{1}$ progressions will similarly reduce to $\hat{3}$–$\hat{1}$, demonstrating that the form of the fundamental line starting from $\hat{3}$ is more fundamental than the form from $\hat{5}$.[44]

The note f^1 is enclosed in square brackets in level *e*, indicating that it no longer plays a role in the voice leading; it may be regarded as a doubling of the soprano's f^2 rather than as an independent voice. Why consider the first tenor a doubling of the soprano, rather than the other way around? Simply because f^2 *is* the soprano. It is the starting point for the principal melodic motions throughout this movement. The first tenor has a certain privileged status because of its interplay with the soprano, but once that interplay is gone—as it is by level *e*—so is the privilege. Textural norms reassert themselves. At this level, therefore, we have only four obbligato voices, not five.

Level *f* shows the prolonged tonic triad. This is the ultimate background level for bars 1–8, but not for the movement as a whole; for the latter, level *f* represents the beginning of the movement's fundamental structure. At level *f*, *only* the outer voices are obbligato; any inner voices belong to the imaginary continuo.

The presence of inner voices (in parentheses) in level *f* is meant to clarify a common misunderstanding. Generally, in graphs of the fundamental structure, inner voices are not shown; one reason for not showing them is that their register cannot be precisely determined. The apparent absence of inner voices from the fundamental structure does not mean, however, that they do not exist; it means only that they have no voice-leading function. This point is widely misunderstood because the fundamental structure appears, on paper, to consist of nothing but a two-voice counterpoint. The existence of inner voices in the fundamental structure is implied by the presence of roman numerals, indicating complete triads.[45]

Example 6.8 exhibited relatively few rhythmic displacements. Example 6.9, from Chopin's "Military" Polonaise (op. 40, no. 1), shows more displacements, including a remarkable one that Schenker analyzed in *Free Composition* (fig. 40,1). The example is presented with a minimum of comment; the reader is encouraged to compare it with Schenker's voice-leading graph.

A difficult analytical decision must be made at the beginning of bar 7: where is the underlying initiation point of II^6? Three possible answers suggest themselves: (1) the downbeat of bar 7, in which case the octave C$^\sharp$ that actually appears there is a kind of suspension to the II^6; (2) the second half of the first beat, where the II^6 first appears on the musical surface; or (3) the second beat of bar 7, in which case the second half of the first beat is heard as an anticipation of II^6. I have chosen the last of these interpretations at level *b*. At level *c*, however, I have chosen the first possibility, hearing the quarter-note C$^\sharp$ of level *b* as a suspension to the II^6 (actually a double suspension, since the bass C$^\sharp$ goes to D while the melody's C$^\sharp$ moves to B). These choices at levels *b* and *c* are not contradictory; they belong to different structural levels, defining an anticipation *within* the resolution of a suspension, rather like the embellished resolutions of fifth-species counterpoint.

It is interesting that the second of the three possible interpretations— that is, taking the rhythmic surface literally—is the least plausible option. This is because nothing in the music heretofore has prepared us for a change of harmony on the weak half of a beat. The harmony has changed at the downbeats of bars 5 and 6; this fact speaks in favor of the interpretation made at level *c*. More local chord changes, as in bars 1, 4, and 5, have always occurred on the strong part of a beat. Bar 4 is especially relevant, because the appoggiatura chord there (a common-tone dimin-

Example 6.9. Chopin, "Military" Polonaise (op. 40, no. 1), reductions of bars 1–8

ished seventh) is analogous to the suspension configuration of bar 7. These precedents readily lead one to interpret the musical surface as in level *b*, even given the ultimate interpretation of level *c*.

The levels starting with *c* are durational reductions. Level *c* reduces the note values of the score by a factor of two and combines Chopin's measures into pairs, reflecting the two-bar level of hypermeter. Levels *d–g*, while retaining the same scale of reduction as level *c*, combine the latter's 6/8 measures into bars of 12/8, thus reflecting the four-bar hypermeter of the excerpt.

Level *c* shows the initial arpeggiation, $c^{\#2}$–e^2–$c^{\#3}$, which is the basis of Schenker's graph. This arpeggiation obviously conflicts with the change of harmony at bar 5. The III$^{\#}$—which actually appears only in bar 6, still supporting $c^{\#3}$ as the structural tone—is ultimately a passing chord within the tonic harmony; this is how Schenker also interprets it. (The actual passing tones, which are best seen at level *d*, are G$^{\#}$ and E$^{\#}$.) Therefore, at a deeper level (represented in example 6.9 by levels *e* and *f*), $c^{\#3}$ appears within the space of the opening tonic harmony. Invoking the rule of arpeggiation leads to the result seen in levels *d–g*, where $c^{\#3}$ appears at the beginning.

Level *b* is formed principally by applying the rule of arpeggiation to level *a*. Level *c* is similarly formed from level *b*. Level *c* indicates that the auxiliary dominant in bar 5 displaces the following III$^{\#}$; the melodic motion in bars 5–6, from C$^{\#}$ to E$^{\#}$ and back again, may thus be interpreted as an arpeggiation within the III$^{\#}$ harmony. (Note that the auxiliary dominant to III$^{\#}$ is metrically accented relative to its resolution, since bar 5 is the first bar of a four-bar hypermeasure.)[46]

The slow harmonic rhythm of bars 1–6 guarantees that normalization following the rule of arpeggiation will yield thick chords in the reduction. These chords can be seen in level *c*. The imaginary continuo for these measures resembles an orchestral texture with a considerable amount of doubling. In fact, one can easily imagine level *c* being used as the basis for an orchestration of the passage. By contrast, the thinner texture of example 6.8, where all voices are obbligato for several levels below the surface (until one gets to level *e*), suggests a very different orchestration for that passage—a far more literal one. Octave doublings or sustained woodwind chords would be inappropriate for the Mozart excerpt; they would be entirely appropriate for the Chopin.

The thinning of the literal texture in bars 7–8 suggests that some voice-leading continuations from bar 6 are merely implied; these are shown in level *c*. Level *d* eliminates all octave doublings, showing only the five obbligato voices. (Notice the parallel octaves C$^{\#}$–D, which are avoided by arpeggiation in the foreground.) It is interesting that the number of obbligato voices here is the same as in bars 1–2 of the Mozart; in the Chopin, however, we have had to eliminate a great deal of octave doubling to arrive at the obbligato texture.

Levels *e* and *f* gradually reduce the progression to the most essential harmonies. The alto voice in level *f* is a composite of the alto and second tenor voices from levels *d* and *e*; these voices exchange the root and fifth of the tonic triad over the course of the excerpt. Notice that, at level *f*, the II harmony reduces out as an appoggiatura chord to the V.

The inner voices of level *f* are basically static: the alto and first tenor have neighboring-note motions to accommodate the V harmony; the second tenor is stationary. Level *g* relegates all inner voices to the imaginary continuo, showing only the prolonged $\hat{3}$ in the soprano. Indeterminate tonic-triad notes fill the space between the outer voices.

Summary

Rhythmic normalization reflects an unconscious process used by every experienced listener in hearing and understanding tonal music. Abnormal or unexpected rhythmic positions of notes and harmonies are continuously compared with the normal or expected positions of the same events. The difference between the normal and abnormal positions represents a measure of rhythmic tension.

Rhythmic normalization depends largely on pitch structure. The most important rule, that of simultaneity (with its corollaries, the rules of arpeggiation and the primary tone), is based on the vertical, harmonic dimension of pitch structure. Purely durational rhythms play a role in rhythmic normalization, but it is a subsidiary role.

Rhythmic normalization also sheds light on questions of texture. Given basic distinctions between obbligato voices, filler tones, and octave doublings, normalization helps one to understand texture as a multi-layered dimension of tonal music, comparable in this respect to rhythm, harmony, and counterpoint.

NOTES

1. See Arthur Komar, *Theory of Suspensions* (Princeton: Princeton University Press, 1971); Peter Westergaard, *An Introduction to Tonal Theory* (New York: W. W. Norton, 1975); Maury Yeston, *The Stratification of Musical Rhythm* (New Haven: Yale University Press, 1976); and Joel Lester, *The Rhythms of Tonal Music* (Carbondale, Ill.: Southern Illinois University Press, 1986). See also the articles by Carl Schachter listed in notes 6 and 15.
2. William Rothstein, "Rhythm and the Theory of Structural Levels" (Ph.D. diss., Yale University, 1981).

3. Fux, *Gradus ad Parnassum*. Reprint of 1725 ed. (New York: Broude Bros., 1966), p. 70. Trans. Alfred Mann, from *Steps to Parnassus: The Study of Counterpoint*, rev. ed. (New York: W. W. Norton, 1965).

4. Note that this is not the only sense in which the term "displacement" is used in music theory. For example, see Arthur Komar's discussion of linear displacement (the replacement of one tone by another within a single line) in his *Theory of Suspensions*.

5. Notice the strong similarity between rhythmic normalization and Schenkerian reduction; the opposite concepts, rhythmic displacement and tonal diminution, are likewise related. As with rhythmic structure, underlying levels of tonal structure (that is, reduction) may be inferred from the musical surface. Conversely, a relatively simple musical passage may be subjected to diminution, yielding a more complex, transformed version of the same passage.

6. See the following two articles by Carl Schachter: "Rhythm and Linear Analysis: Durational Reduction," in Felix Salzer and Carl Schachter, eds., *The Music Forum*, vol. 5 (New York: Columbia University Press, 1980), pp. 197–232; and "Rhythm and Linear Analysis: Aspects of Meter," in Felix Salzer and Carl Schachter, eds., *The Music Forum*, vol. 6, pt. 1 (New York: Columbia University Press, 1987), pp. 1–59. See also William Rothstein's *Phrase Rhythm in Tonal Music* (New York: Schirmer Books, 1990).

   At the 1987 meeting of the Society for Music Theory (Rochester, N.Y.), Charles Burkhart presented a paper on the rhythmic analysis of passages from Mozart's operas.

7. See chapters 2 and 3 of Rothstein, *Phrase Rhythm in Tonal Music*.

8. For an application of the same principle to prolongational structure in tonal music, see Fred Lerdahl and Ray Jackendoff, *A Generative Theory of Tonal Music* (Cambridge, Mass.: MIT Press, 1983), pp. 179–249.

9. The concept I am propounding here, of a fluctuating distance between musical surface and underlying norm, is closely related to Lerdahl and Jackendoff's "depth of embedding." What is new is my claim that the concept applies as much to the rhythmic domain as it does to prolongational pitch structure.

10. See Yeston, *The Stratification of Musical Rhythm*.

11. On accented neighboring and passing tones, see Edward Aldwell and Carl Schachter, *Harmony and Voice Leading*, vol. 2 (New York: Harcourt Brace Jovanovich, 1979), p. 12.

12. If there were a change of harmony under the G—say, a C-major triad changing to a G-major triad—the E of the first measure might be understood to move by step to another implied pitch (D in this case).

13. Westergaard, *An Introduction to Tonal Theory*; see his discussion of the "law of segmentation," pp. 228–232.

14. See Rothstein, "Rhythm and the Theory of Structural Levels," pp. 36–39.

15. Carl Schachter, "Rhythm and Linear Analysis: A Preliminary Study," in Felix Salzer and Carl Schachter, eds., *The Music Forum*, vol. 4 (New York: Columbia University Press, 1976), pp. 281–334.

16. Schenker, *Free Composition*, trans. and ed. Ernst Oster (New York: Schirmer Books, 1979). See p. 105 and fig. 125.

17. Ibid., fig. 125,1. See also Rothstein, "Rhythm and the Theory of Structural Levels," pp. 28–31 and 78.

18. Harmonic intervals are most often consonant, but they may be dissonant in the case of seventh chords.

19. See the discussion of harmonic rhythm in Edward Aldwell and Carl Schachter, *Harmony and Voice Leading*, vol. 1 (New York: Harcourt Brace Jovanovich, 1978), pp. 83–84. Note that the continuation of a harmony from a strong beat through a weak beat to another strong beat is not at issue here.

20. See Aldwell and Schachter, *Harmony and Voice Leading*, 2:7, 17, and 39–40.

21. Schenker, *Free Composition*, pp. 56–57. See also 58–60.

22. I am currently preparing a series of essays that explores the "imaginary continuo" in detail.

23. Schenker, "The Largo of J. S. Bach's Sonata No. 3 for Unaccompanied Violin," trans. John Rothgeb, in Felix Salzer and Carl Schachter, eds., *The Music Forum*, vol. 4 (New York: Columbia University Press, 1976), p. 153.

   An interesting recent study is Alan Lessem's "Schumann's Arrangements of Bach as Reception History," in *Journal of Musicological Research* 7 (1986): 29–46. Lessem details some of the ways in which Schumann's arrangements exceed the function of filling in the imaginary continuo (he does not use that term, of course). Lessem's conclusions are slightly skewed, however, by his focus on the Chaconne from the Partita No. 2 (D minor); Schumann's accompaniment to the Chaconne is unusually elaborate.

24. This motion could conceivably be thought of as a descending register transfer from $c^{\sharp 2}$ to d^1, but I consider this an inferior interpretation because of the longer-range significance of $c^{\sharp 2}$. The latter tone remains in effect in the voice leading until the third bar of example 6.5, where it moves to d^2 in parallel tenths with Schumann's "tenor."

25. Schumann's piano part also does not take explicit notice of Bach's descending third-progression $f^{\sharp 2}$–e^2–d^2. However, in the larger context of the piece this motion is subordinate to the motion from $c^{\sharp 2}$ (bar 1) to d^2 (bar 3).

26. In Schenker's graphs, the displacement of the primary tone from the

initial tonic bass note is shown by means of a diagonal line connecting the two notes. This graphic device, however, shows only the *fact* of displacement. It does not show the *direction* of displacement (does the bass anticipate, or is the soprano delayed?). Nor can it show the underlying initiation point of the vertical chord that results from normalization.

27. If II^6 is substituted for IV in this progression, the common-tone feature is partly lost. However, the connective bass arpeggiation, by outlining IV, actually stresses the substitute nature of II^6; the $\hat{2}$ of II^6 will be heard as an upper-neighbor embellishment of $\hat{1}$.

28. See Schenker, *Free Composition*, p. 113.

29. See Rothstein, "Rhythm and the Theory of Structural Levels," pp. 84–86. This principle, which also holds for secondary V–I progressions, applies only when V is an auxiliary chord. Thus it does not apply when V–I is the goal of a cadential progression beginning with the tonic.

30. See Schachter, "Rhythm and Linear Analysis: A Preliminary Study," p. 302.

31. See Schenker, *Free Composition*, pp. 88–89; also Rothstein, "Rhythm and the Theory of Structural Levels," pp. 122–128. If a V–I auxiliary cadence takes place within a single metrical unit (e.g., a hypermeasure) in which the V appears on the downbeat, this principle does not apply. Rather, the V is understood to delay the I as described earlier (see note 29).

32. Schenker himself was somewhat equivocal about the status of seventh chords. See William Clark, "Heinrich Schenker on the Nature of the Seventh Chord," *Journal of Music Theory* 26, 2 (1982): 221–259.

33. See Schenker, *Harmony*, ed. Oswald Jonas, trans. Elisabeth Mann Borgese (Chicago: University of Chicago Press, 1954 and 1980), pp. 133ff. and 211ff.

34. See note 31. Neither passage in example 6.6 involves real conflict between melodic and harmonic prolongations, because in each case the local tonic—which is the harmony being prolonged in both dimensions—has been established earlier; the passage shown is thus merely part of a longer prolongation. Several cases involving real prolongational conflict are shown in *Free Composition*, fig. 110, including examples a3, c1, c2, and d3.

35. Schenker, *Das Meisterwerk in der Musik* (3 vols.; Munich: Drei Masken Verlag, 1925, 1926, 1930 [reissued as 3 vols. in 1 slightly reduced facsimile, Hildesheim: Olms, 1974]), vol. 2, p. 15.

36. Ibid. For a discussion of Schenker's term *Kopfton* and its various translations, see Rothstein, "Rhythm and the Theory of Structural Levels," pp. 94–96. I use the term "primary tone" to mean *the tone of highest*

structural value in a linear progression, whether that is the first tone or the last.

37. Schenker, *Free Composition*, pp. 45–46.
38. The distinction between obbligato voices and filler tones, which assumes additional importance in the analytical portion of this essay, is taken from Schenker; see especially his unpublished treatise *Die Kunst des Vortrags*.
39. See Schenker, *Free Composition*, pp. 31–32 and figs. 15–16.
40. These and related subjects are discussed in Rothstein's *Phrase Rhythm in Tonal Music*.
41. This notational device is introduced in Schachter, "Rhythm and Linear Analysis: Durational Reduction" (see full citation in note 6).
42. In Schenker's voice-leading graphs, where rhythm and meter are not specified (except at foreground levels), rhythmic normalization is indicated by the relative alignment of notes *between* levels. (See "Rhythm and the Theory of Structural Levels," pp. 81–82 and 97–100.) Thus my analytical procedure is not very different from Schenker's, although mine is more explicit and somewhat more systematic.
43. Schachter, "Rhythm and Linear Analysis: Durational Reduction," p. 232.
44. This is not an original observation. Some theorists—Joel Lester, for example (private conversation)—have even maintained that a piece's fundamental line *cannot* start from $\hat{5}$ but only from $\hat{3}$. I reject this conclusion, but agree that the $\hat{5}$-line belongs conceptually to a slightly later level than the $\hat{3}$-line in the evolution from the ultimate background (the tonic triad itself) toward the foreground.
45. See Schenker, *Free Composition*, fig. 1.
46. See note 29.

Hidden Uses of Chorale Melodies in Bach's Cantatas

David Stern

The central role of Lutheran chorale melodies in Bach's sacred music is well known.[1] These melodies are incorporated into every form of vocal music used by Bach, not only in the four-part harmonizations and in the great opening chorale fantasias, but also in arias, ariosos, and recitatives. One of Bach's compositional practices was to alternate recitative passages with the phrases of a chorale melody; another was to combine chorale melodies with seemingly independent compositions. An outstanding example of this procedure is the use of "O Lamm Gottes" in the opening chorus of the *St. Matthew Passion*, one-third of the way through the movement. Another example is "Mein teurer Heiland" from the *St. John Passion*, in which an entire four-part chorale harmonization is superimposed over a bass aria. In short, Bach used the chorale melodies with inexhaustible ingenuity and variety in his sacred vocal music.

Since the chorale melodies are used in such a variety of forms, it is not surprising that they appear in different guises. They may be quoted literally or appear in ornamented form. Furthermore, motivic material is often derived from them, and structural features of chorale melodies are at times incorporated into choruses and arias without the chorale melody actually being quoted. The more extensive expansions of chorale tunes and the use of a chorale tune's structure without actual quotation have not been fully explored in modern scholarship. This essay focuses primarily on these aspects of Bach's compositional practice. Its purpose is not only to show specific examples, but also to demonstrate that the scope of Bach's compositional treatment of chorale melodies is greater than has been generally recognized, ranging from literal quotation to complex large-scale expansions.

The importance of the chorale melodies in Bach's everyday life is reflected in Forkel's description of Bach's meetings with his relatives, at which "the first thing they did, when they were assembled, was to sing a chorale. From this pious commencement they proceeded to drolleries which often made a very great contrast with it."[2] Furthermore, Carl Philipp Emanuel Bach relates that his father taught chorale harmonization as one of the basic skills in composition:

> He [J. S. Bach] started his pupils right in with what was practical, and omitted all the *dry species* of counterpoint that are given in Fux and others. His pupils had to begin their studies by learning pure four-part thorough bass. From this he went to chorales; first he added the basses to them himself, and they had to invent the alto and tenor. Then he taught them to devise the basses themselves. (C. P. E. Bach's italics)[3]

Bach's pupil Kirnberger considered the chorale melody to form a basic model from which more elaborate melodies could be derived. In his treatise *Die Kunst des reinen Satzes in der Musik* Kirnberger writes:

> For the benefit of the beginner of composition we cannot let go unmentioned here that at most a diligent training in chorales is a highly useful and even indispensable matter, and that those who consider such exercises as superfluous or even pedantic are caught in a very detrimental bias. Such exercises are the true foundation not only of strict composition but also for good and proper expression in vocal compositions.
>
> Every aria is basically nothing more than a chorale composed according to the most correct declamation, in which each syllable of the text has only one note, which is more or less embellished according to the demands of expression. The true basis of beauty in an aria always depends on the simple melody that is left when all its decorative notes are eliminated. If this simple melody is incorrect in terms of declamation, progression, or harmony, mistakes cannot be completely hidden by embellishment.
>
> Whoever wants to take pains to strip the most beautiful arias of all embellishments will see that the remaining notes always have the shape of a well-composed and correctly declaimed chorale.[4]

Kirnberger then gives excerpts from two arias in which he reduces the original melodies to simpler, chorale-like versions; the first of these is presented in example 7.1. The original melody (an aria from the opera *Tamerlano* by Graun) appears in the upper staff, and Kirnberger's chorale-like reduction is placed in the staff below it.

Kirnberger's reductive examples form a counterpart to the more prevalent theoretical tradition of presenting examples of simple melodic ideas that are embellished, a tradition that goes back to the pre-Baroque period.[5] Given Kirnberger's demonstration of the relation between chorale-like melodies and aria melodies, it is hardly surprising that actual chorale melodies were used as a point of departure for arias in cantata movements, even in highly elaborate settings where the melodic material of the aria

Example 7.1. From Kirnberger, *The Art of Strict Musical Composition*

is embellished and far from the simple style of chorale tunes. The same practice was extended to choruses and recitatives. It may be added that Mattheson gives various examples of chorale melodies transformed into various types of dances (for example, the bourrée and the polonaise).[6] Example 7.2 is taken from Mattheson's treatise *Der vollkommene Cappell-meister*, and it shows the chorale melody "Werde munter, mein Gemüte" used as a bourrée melody. Thus, the idea of altering and embellishing chorale melodies was well grounded in the theory and aesthetics of the age.

The presence of ornamented chorale melodies in Bach's cantatas has been reported by various scholars including Philipp Spitta, Hubert Parry, Hugo Goldschmidt, and Hermann Sirp.[7] Among these authors, Sirp gives the most extensive and systematic exposition of the subject, and provides examples of Bach's use of chorale melodies (in either literal or varied form) in choruses, arias, and recitatives. Two examples from Sirp's study are shown in example 7.3. Example 7.3a, from the single-movement cho-

Example 7.2. Chorale melody and Bourrée

Example 7.3. Paraphrased chorale melodies

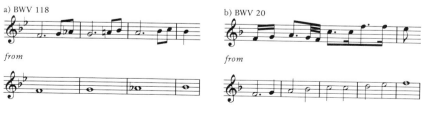

rale cantata "O Jesu Christ, mein's Lebens Licht" (BWV 118), shows Bach's simple embellishment of the chorale melody. Example 7.3b, from the opening chorale fantasia "O Ewigkeit, du Donnerwort" (BWV 20), presents a different technique. Here the chorale melody is not literally embellished; rather, a new melodic idea is derived from the octave ascent of the chorale. In other words, this melodic idea is derived from a structural aspect of the chorale melody.[8]

Sirp also points out that the famous triplet melody from the chorale setting that concludes both sections of Cantata 147 is a variation of "Werde munter, mein Gemüte"; we have already encountered this chorale tune in example 7.2.[9] The melody is quoted in example 7.4, which is from Dürr's monograph on the cantatas of Bach.[10] Unlike Sirp, Dürr shows an analysis, a specific alignment between the chorale as sung in the soprano part and the notes of the triplet melody. This is a wonderful example of how Bach could adhere to the structure of a chorale tune while creating a new and exceptionally inspired melody. The structure of this melody and its relevance to Cantata 147 as a whole is discussed later.

Since chorale melodies are often disguised by figuration, it is hardly surprising that their presence in specific movements from Bach's cantatas has sometimes been overlooked. The Terzetto "Wenn meine Trübsal als mit Ketten" from the cantata "Aus tiefer Not schrei' ich zu dir" (BWV 38) does not quote the chorale tune literally at any point, but contains a reference to it which has gone unnoticed because it is somewhat more hidden than those cited in Sirp's study.[11] Bach's figured bass, a realization, and the notes of the chorale melody are given in example 7.5.

A particularly fascinating aspect of this example is the voice-leading requirement that the b♭ in bar 3 be understood as moving to the a in bar 4, since the b♭ is the lowest note of a $^6_4$ chord that requires resolution by a downward step. The same applies for the notes a and g in bars 4–7; thus,

Example 7.4. BWV 147, VI, derivation of ritornello from the chorale melody

Example 7.5. BWV 38, Terzetto, derivation of bass from chorale melody

there emerges an underlying line descending from b♭ to f in bars 2–8 that is clearly derived from the chorale melody (see the asterisks in example 7.5). The ascending-sixth leap from d to b♭ in bars 1–2 is derived from the rising sixth outlined in the second to fourth notes of the chorale. Furthermore, this sixth is echoed by the subsequent rising sixths, as shown by the brackets in example 7.5. Bach thus derives the figuration for this elaboration of the chorale melody from a striking feature of the chorale itself (see also the bracket in bar 2, which shows that the chorale forms the basis of the right-hand figuration).

It is obvious that the chorale melody is not actually quoted in the Terzetto; rather, it forms the basis for a new idea. The original Phrygian mode of the melody, which is preserved in the opening and closing choruses of the cantata, is reinterpreted as modern D minor. The presence of the chorale melody in the Terzetto—albeit in veiled form—means that every movement of the cantata (except for the first recitative) either cites the chorale tune or alludes to it. The chorale tune thus forms a musically unifying element running through the cantata as a whole; that one recitative does not allude to the tune is not sufficient to weaken the overriding musical unity. Indeed, since recitatives function as connecting interludes in which word declamation plays a primary role, it is not surprising that they do not always quote or refer to the chorale melody even when all the arias and choruses do. Of course, the practice of using a chorale melody to unify a cantata did not originate with Bach; it is found far more openly in the traditional form known as the cantata "per omnes versus," in which the strophes of a chorale are set as independent movements, thus forming a series of variations on the chorale melody, as in Bach's "Christ lag in Todesbanden" (BWV 4).

Example 7.5 also illustrates a special aspect of the unifying procedure discussed above. When Bach created a motive from a chorale melody, he usually derived it from the opening notes or phrase of the tune.[12] One reason undoubtedly is that the opening tends to be the most recognizable and characteristic part of the chorale melody; another is that, in Bach's style, only a few notes are necessary to create motives suitable for repetition and development. One can easily see that an attempt to derive motivic material for an aria from an entire chorale melody would be impractical, particulary if the melody was to be expanded by embellishments. The only types of compositions to systematically develop entire chorale melodies are chorale fantasias or chorale preludes in which the accompanying voices derive their motives from each new line of the cantus firmus, in the manner of Pachelbel.[13] However, if a motive was to be expanded on a large scale, Bach's characteristic procedure was to derive the new idea from the opening of the chorale, and then proceed to develop the new melodic line just as he would with any freely invented motive. This is the case with the remaining chorale-derived motives that are discussed in this paper.

A different aspect of "Aus tiefer Not schrei' ich zu dir" remains to be discussed, namely, its symbolic meaning. A common liturgical theme in Bach's cantatas is the portrayal of an initial struggle that is later resolved by the promise of salvation. Cantata 38 follows this outline: it opens with the cry "Out of the depths of need," and progresses to the comforting words of the Terzetto and the final chorale setting, which tell of God's mercy. Surely, then, the allusion to the chorale in the Terzetto heightens the sense that the initial cry of despair has been answered in an optimistic light.

Bach's use of motivic expansion, or hidden enlargement, deserves special mention.[14] This compositional procedure, uncovered by Schenker, is an important unifying procedure found in the masterworks that Schenker studied in such exhaustive depth. Motivic expansion involves recomposing an idea, which normally appears on or near the surface of a composition, over a span that may extend from a few measures to an entire section, or even more. In a fully integrated composition, it is logical that large-scale ideas should grow out of ideas on the surface. Since the expansion of basic melodic ideas was a procedure often used by Bach, it is not surprising that the technique of hidden enlargement was applied to chorale melodies. In such cases, the chorale is sometimes used within a movement in both literal and expanded form, while at other times, as in the Terzetto, it is present only in expanded form. In movements utilizing chorales either in direct quotation or in hidden form, other motivic ideas, not directly derived from the chorale, may also be subject to hidden expansion. The procedure thus varies in many ways from piece to piece, and its particular manifestation can be determined only by the analysis of individual movements.

Example 7.5 illustrates the expansion of a chorale melody that is on a somewhat broader scope than has been generally represented in Bach scholarship. The opening movement of "Es reisset euch ein schrecklich Ende" (BWV 90) also contains an expansion of a chorale phrase that is removed from the surface of the composition. Here, the material is drawn from the first phrase of the chorale "Nimm von uns, Herr, du treuer Gott" by Martin Moller (1584). An analysis of the ritornello from the opening movement appears in example 7.6. As in the Terzetto from Cantata 38, the opening phrase of the chorale melody—a^1–a^1–f^1–g^1–a^1–f^1–e^1–d^1—is enlarged in the ritornello, but not literally quoted.

In accordance with the *Affekt* of the text, which tells of the terrible fate that awaits sinners, the music is dramatic, in the style of an Italian concerto, far removed from the world of the four-voice chorale harmonization. The way the chorale theme unfolds in this movement is quite

Example 7.6. BWV 90, I, ritornello, opening bars and analytical sketches fascinating. Before any element directly relating to the chorale tune enters, an entirely new idea is introduced in the first violin part: the neighbor note figure d^2–$c^{\sharp2}$–d^2 followed by a descending arpeggio from d^2 to d^1 (example 7.6a). In these bars the chorale's initial skip of a descending third, a^1–f^1, is elaborated by an upper neighbor note $b^{\flat1}$ and a stepwise descent to f^1: a^1–$b^{\flat1}$–a^1–g^1–f^1 (the brackets in example 7.6c show two preliminary statements of this chorale-derived tone succession in bars 1–6).

In bars 8–9, the upper neighbor note $b^{\flat1}$ is given greater duration and moves through a dramatic rising scale to a^2, the first note of the chorale tune expansion (bar 11), which now appears prominently as the highest note heard so far. In bars 11–18, the uppermost notes clearly outline the contour of the opening phrase of the chorale melody (see the asterisks in examples 7.6b and 7.6c). The way in which the chorale elaboration emerges (bars 11–18) from its "germinal" form (bars 1–6) is quite beautiful; here we see a chorale tune being transformed to create a particularly dramatic effect. The f^2 that arrives over dominant harmony in bar 16 is displaced; it is an anticipation, properly belonging to the following $B^\flat$ harmony in bar 17, as example 7.6c shows. An unexpected arrival on a first inversion D-major chord (bar 18) in place of the expected root position D-minor harmony is followed by halting rhythms and dissonant harmonies. Clearly, the events in bars 18–20 depict the terrible fate of the sinner.[15]

In a symbolic sense, the music is operating on two levels. On one level, there is the obvious dramatic depiction of the dire fate of the sinner; on another, there is the hidden use of a chorale melody which is later sung to the words "Lead us with your right hand." The duality of levels is significant, for, in effect, it shows that divine order is all pervasive and dominates even when it is not apparent—in this case, on the ground that the sinner walks.

In contrast to Cantata 38, only the first and last movements of Cantata 90 draw on the chorale melody. The degree to which chorale melodies help unify Bach's cantatas obviously varies from case to case. Furthermore, Bach's ability to transform a chorale melody to underlie an entirely different piece of music was quite remarkable. It seems unlikely that he worked out the chorale melody's transformation note by note; rather, the new music probably sprang up more or less spontaneously under the guiding impetus provided by the chorale melody.

In the examples from Cantata 38 and Cantata 90, the chorale elaborations go somewhat beyond the limits of simple paraphrase technique. However, in both cases the voice leading does reduce to a fairly literal rendition of the chorale melody, and the underlying melody's notes are not so widely separated, appearing within one or two measures of one another, so that the ear can follow the progress of the chorale tune without great difficulty. The procedure in these cases might well be called "expanded paraphrase technique." Bach's ability to coordinate musical ideas on a vast scale, however, enabled him to compose even more far-reaching expansions in which it is no longer possible to speak of paraphrase technique. In such expansions, the melody is not literally quoted; rather, structural features from its opening are incorporated into the large-scale voice leading. These large-scale expansions typically occur in orchestral introductions or ritornellos; the chorale melody itself may appear afterwards in the vocal section.

To the best of my knowledge, Heinrich Schenker was the first musician to write about such a large-scale expansion of the structure of a chorale melody in Bach. In a brilliant essay in *Der Tonwille* on the opening chorus of the *St. Matthew Passion*, Schenker showed that the structure of the chorale melody "O Lamm Gottes" is composed-out on a vast scale in the opening orchestral introduction.[16] Since the opening chorus is in E minor, the G-major structure of the chorale melody is transposed to E minor in its initial hidden statement. This expansion prepares for the later dramatic entry of the chorale tune, which is thereby integrated into the movement as a whole.

Large-scale expansion of a similar nature occurs in the ritornello of the opening chorus from the cantata "Wachet auf, ruft uns die Stimme" (BWV 140). The chorale melody begins with an arpeggiated rising fifth followed by an upper neighbor note ($\hat{1}$–$\hat{3}$–$\hat{5}$–$\hat{6}$–$\hat{5}$); the expansion of this melodic idea in the ritornello of the opening movement is shown in the voice-leading reduction of example 7.7.[17] In addition to the expansion, the ritornello contains numerous rising triadic figures that are obvious references to the chorale's opening notes, and which are well known (see the first violin and bass parts, bars 6ff.).

The expansion of the chorale melody in the upper voice includes both the rising triad ($e^{\flat 2}$–g^2–$b^{\flat 2}$) and the upper neighbor note c^3 (see the asterisks in example 7.7). It is interesting to note that precisely at the completion of the expanded rising triad the design changes and the rhythm

Example 7.7. BWV 140, I, ritornello, analytical sketch

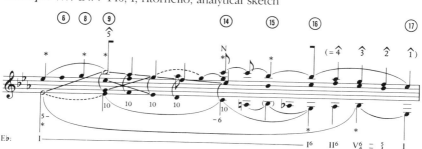

becomes more animated. The increased momentum leads to the arrival on the upper neighbor note c³ in the first violin part (bar 14), which stands out as the highest note of the ritornello; the return from c³ to b♭² (in the first violin part, bar 16) is likewise emphasized by another significant change in design. At the same time, the bass shows an expanded rising triadic structure (see the asterisks under the bass line in example 7.7) that is related to the opening of the chorale melody, although in itself the bass does not form as clear an expansion of the chorale incipit as is found in the upper voice. The opening of the chorale tune thus pervades the entire ritornello and progresses through various musical layers that overlap but move at various rates of motion, in both small and large dimensions.

The fourth movement of Cantata 140 is one of Bach's most famous compositions (example 7.8). Discussions of its remarkable opening melody have emphasized its markedly different nature from that of the chorale tune. Schweitzer calls it "a simple dance melody" with which "the chorale is combined dissonantly, as if it had nothing to do with it."[18] Sirp classifies this movement as one in which the chorale melody is contrasted with a self-sufficient motive that is not derived from the chorale tune itself.[19]

It is true that the unison string melody does not outwardly derive its motivic material from the chorale. We hear a new melody, with its own motives; in particular, rising and descending third-motives predominate throughout (many of the larger thirds are shown in example 7.8). The question arises, though, of whether a composer so accustomed to integrating musical ideas would compose a new theme simply to provide an effective counterpoint to the chorale melody. Is there not a deeper relationship between them? A musical connection between them does in fact exist: the structural melodic motion in bars 1–5 is an ascent from e♭¹, on the initial downbeat, to b♭¹, with g¹ serving as the principal intermediary note. The arrival on b♭¹ is given emphasis by the return to *forte*.[20] This upward arpeggio is accompanied by far more obvious references in the

Example 7.8. BWV 140, IV, ritornello, analytical sketch

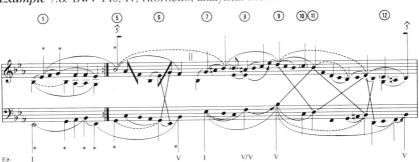

bass to the rising triad of the chorale incipit (bars 1–2 and bars 3–4; compare the similar E♭–G–B♭ bass motion at the beginning of the cantata's concluding chorale setting). These patterns are embraced by an expanded repetition of the chorale incipit that unfolds across bars 1–6 (example 7.8; see the asterisks in the bass).

All three chorale movements in Cantata 140, then, use the chorale melody's rising arpeggio motivically. Also, the two arias contain bass lines that arpeggiate upward by thirds from tonic to dominant. To be sure, such basses are common enough, but in the context of the present cantata they seem to take on an added motivic meaning, namely, a reference to the chorale. If one accepts these rising fifths in the arias as references to the chorale tune, it may then be said that the chorale tune unifies the cantata as a whole.

The final work to be discussed here is "Herz und Mund und Tat und Leben" (BWV 147). The cantata is in two parts; both parts end with musically identical settings of two strophes from the chorale melody shown in example 7.2, "Werde munter, mein Gemüte." Dürr's analysis of the relationship of the triplet melody to the chorale tune has been presented above in example 7.4. I should like to discuss the way in which Bach harmonizes the chorale melody, for this sheds light on structural characteristics to be found throughout the remaining arias and choruses of the cantata.

For convenience, let us consider the chorale setting at the end of the first section of the sixth movement, which begins with the words "Wohl mir, dass ich Jesum habe" (example 7.9; the asterisks again indicate the embedded chorale tune).[21] A study of the relationship between the melody and its harmonization shows that the melodic line descends from $\hat{3}$, since there are no strong harmonic progressions to support a structural descent from $\hat{5}$, particularly in the antecedent phrases (bars 1–4 and 9–12). Furthermore, the chorale tune as given by Mattheson clearly descends from $\hat{3}$, because $\hat{4}$ does not support a descent from $\hat{5}$ in the consequent phrases (see bar 2 in example 7.2).

There are also strong motivic reasons for reading the upper voice as descending from $\hat{3}$. The reading in example 7.9 shows that the second antecedent phrase (bars 9–12) contains an ascending third followed by a descending third; indeed, the chorale tune is almost entirely fashioned from this melodic figure. Bach interpolated further versions of the motive in his ornaments of the melody, an instance of which is presented in example 7.10. Thus, an analysis which reads the upper voice from $\hat{3}$ proves most satisfactory in regard to the tonal structure, motivic design, and faithfulness to the original chorale tune.

In composing a new melody from a chorale tune, it was common for Bach also to introduce a new motive; we have seen that the third-motive

Example 7.9. BWV 147, VI, analytical sketches

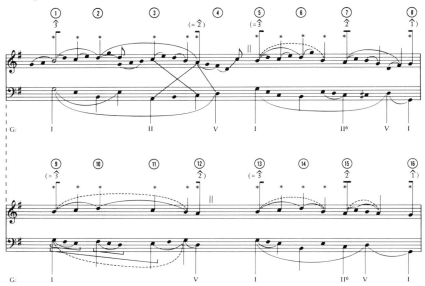

Example 7.10. BWV 147, VI, rising-falling third-motive

played an important role as an accompaniment to the rising arpeggio in the fourth movement of Cantata 140 (example 7.8). In the present movement, third-motives again play a primary role, and bars 9–11 contain a particularly interesting motivic development: as the brackets under the bass indicate (example 7.9), the smaller descending third of bar 9 is expanded in the larger bass motion in bars 9–11. Furthermore, the motion back to g in the bass completes an arch that mirrors the upper voice.

The chorale melody is not quoted literally in any of the arias or in the opening chorus, but a structural outline derived from it appears in each of those movements. Example 7.11 illustrates this outline, the melodic contour of which is derived from the consequent phrase of the chorale tune (note the ascending and descending thirds). Bach fashioned entirely new music for the opening chorus and arias, with the guiding structural outline often present, so that in a hidden way, the cantata is unified by the chorale melody.

The structural outline shown in example 7.11 is transformed in the glorious ritornello of the opening chorus, the beginning of which is pre-

Example 7.11. BWV 147, structural outline from "Werde munter. mein Gemüte"

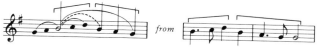

sented in example 7.12. The main motive from the chorale melody, the ascending third followed by a descending third, is stated almost immediately in the first measure, and it also appears in expanded form in bars 1–2 (see the brackets in example 7.12 and the additional references to the motive shown in the second part of the example).

The voice leading of the entire ritornello follows the structural outline shown in example 7.11, although in greatly expanded form (example 7.13). As in the triplet melody to the final chorus, the note that corresponds to the initial note of the chorale melody, $\hat{3}$, is preceded by an ascending third from $\hat{1}$ that establishes the primary tone $\hat{3}$ on the downbeats of bars 2 and 3. In bars 3–7, the trumpet plays an ascending third from e^2 to g^2 that is answered by g^2 to e^2 over a larger span: the second motion is extended through a subordinate descending third that works out a^2 as an incomplete upper neighbor to g^2. The brackets in example 7.13 show the pattern of this motive and its subsequent expansion.

The upper voice, beginning in bar 2, is supported by a bass that moves by descending fifths. Although bars 7–8 contain an accelerated version of bars 3–5, the musical context suggests a different interpretation of the same succession of harmonies, as example 7.13 indicates. In the second

Example 7.12. BWV 147, I, ritornello

Example 7.13. BWV 147, I, ritornello, analytical sketches

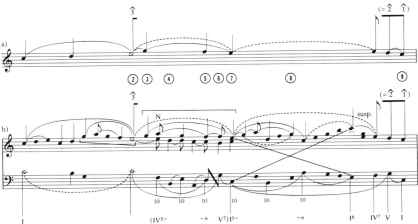

case, the descending fifth-progression occurs within a larger voice ex-change that expands tonic harmony and establishes c³ as the climax of the ritornello, which then moves quickly to e² over the IV⁷ chord in bar 8. This tone is a suspension of the primary tone 3̂, whose resolution initiates the final motion to 1̂ that achieves tonal closure for the ritornello and completes the structural outline derived from the chorale. Thus the ger-minal melodic figure of the chorale melody (the ascending and descending third) is used extensively from the very beginning of the cantata, at the surface and foreground and at deeper levels of the structure.

The ritornello provides a striking illustration of Bach's genius for creating musically integrated compositions: the larger voice leading springs up in the most organic way from the surface motives. Since the motives are derived from the chorale, the ritornello mirrors the chorale in countless ways. The chorale underlies virtually every note in one way or another, and on more than one level at a time.

The pervasive influence of the chorale-derived structural outline throughout Cantata 147 also unifies the ritornellos of the third, fifth, and ninth movements; moreover, the motive of an ascending third followed by a descending third occurs on or very near the surface in the opening measures of each of these movements. In order to illustrate this, let us briefly consider the ritornello of the third movement, an analysis of which is presented in example 7.14. The point here is that the structural outline influences the large-scale structure, and the surface motive from which the outline is derived occurs at the foreground throughout the ritornello. Note that the structural outline is slightly different in example 7.14, be-ginning with a rising sixth in place of the usual third (which appears in the first, fifth, and ninth movements).

Example 7.14. BWV 147, III, ritornello, analytical sketches

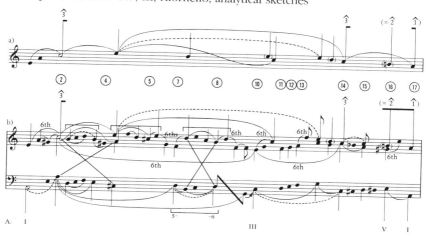

The seventh movement reveals a somewhat different case. Here, its ritornello seems to be derived from the famous triplet melody of the sixth movement (example 7.15; for comparison, a transposed version of the famous triplet melody is presented on the upper stave). Specifically, the last four notes of the sixth movement occur transposed as the first four notes of the seventh movement; furthermore, the same motivic figure also appears in various guises throughout the fifth, sixth, and seventh movements (example 7.16). Hence a more immediate kind of motivic integration unifies these movements at surface and foreground levels.

It is interesting to see how such closely related underlying structures are expressed through the particular types of figuration found in each of these movements. Through these figurations, motivic ideas arise on or near the surface; we have seen that third-motives permeate the various structural levels of the first and sixth movements of Cantata 147. Since the

Example 7.15. BWV 147, VII, ritornello, analytical sketch

Example *7.16.* BWV 147, a recurrent melodic figure

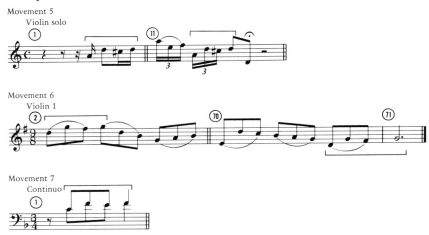

chorale tune consists so largely of thirds, we can see Bach's setting of "Wohl mir, dass ich Jesum habe" as an intensification of the inner characteristics of the chorale tune. In other movements, the motives may be less directly related in order to create their individual natures. The reader may wish to explore this further; here, I shall mention only the importance of the interval of the sixth in the third and seventh movements, and of the fourth in the ninth movement.

This study has presented specific examples of chorale-melody expansions in Bach cantatas, and has shown that Bach's adoption of Lutheran chorale tunes was even farther reaching than has been shown in previous studies of his cantatas. We have seen that the use of these tunes may extend far beyond an elaborate paraphrasing, and that the tune may penetrate to deep levels of musical structure. Future studies will surely reveal further profoundly inspired transformations of chorale melodies in Bach's cantatas; the interested musician may wish "to take pains to strip the most beautiful arias of all embellishments," to see whether the underlying notes have the shape of a chorale.

Bach's far-reaching transformations of chorale melodies in his cantatas clearly point to the great spiritual significance that these tunes had for him. It is easy for the modern listener to be dazzled by the complexity of the opening choruses, arias, and recitatives, and to think of the final chorale harmonization as relatively modest. However, these chorale harmonizations represent Bach's religious expression distilled to its purest and most direct form. In this sense, the closing chorale harmonizations represent the climax toward which Bach's sacred cantatas unfold.

NOTES

1. A shorter version of this essay was read at the Society for Music Theory Conference at Indiana University in November, 1986. I wish to thank Professors Carl Schachter and George Stauffer of CUNY and Mr. Channan Willner for their valuable suggestions for this study. The *Neue Bach Ausgabe* was used for the analyses of the following cantatas: BWV 38, BWV 90, and BWV 140; the *Bach Gesellschaft* was used for BWV 147.

2. This passage is translated in *The Bach Reader*, rev. ed., ed. Hans T. David and Arthur Mendel (New York: W. W. Norton, 1966), pp. 300–301.

3. Ibid., p. 279.

4. Johann Philipp Kirnberger, *Die Kunst des reinen Satzes in der Musik* (Berlin, 1771–1779), partial trans. David Beach and Jürgen Thym as *The Art of Strict Musical Composition* (New Haven: Yale University Press, 1982), pp. 233–234.

5. For an example from Bach's period, see Johann Mattheson, *Der vollkommene Capellmeister* (Hamburg, 1739); facsimile ed. (Kassel: Bärenreiter, 1954), pt. 2, ch. 3. Hermann Sirp points to this theoretical tradition and cites examples from this chapter in Mattheson in "Die Thematik der Kirchenkantaten J. S. Bachs in ihren Beziehungen zum protestantischen Kirchenlied," *Bach-Jahrbuch* 28 (1931): 1–50, and *Bach-Jahrbuch* 29 (1932): 51–118 (see especially pp. 4ff.).

6. Mattheson, *Der vollkommene Capellmeister*, pt. 2, ch. 6. Mattheson's transformations of chorales into dances are discussed by Sirp in "Die Thematic in der Kirchenkanten J. S. Bachs," pp. 8–9.

7. Philipp Spitta, *Johann Sebastian Bach*, trans. Clara Bell and J. A. Fuller-Maitland (London: Novello, 1889; reprint, New York: Dover Publications, 1952), vol. 1, p. 616. C. Hubert H. Parry, *Johann Sebastian Bach*, rev. ed. (London: Putnam, 1927), pp. 272 and 280–282, as well as further references in chs. 11–12. Hugo Goldschmidt, "Die Anführung von Kirchenmelodien in den Mittelteilen der J. S. Bachschen Kantaten," *Zeitschrift für Musikwissenschaft* 2 (1920): 392–399 (see especially 398). Sirp, "Die Thematik der Kirchenkantaten J. S. Bachs," contains numerous examples throughout.

8. Sirp, "Die Thematik der Kirchenkantaten J. S. Bachs," pp. 84 (example 7.3a), and 83 (example 7.3b).

9. Ibid., p. 75.

10. Alfred Dürr, *Die Kantaten von Johann Sebastian Bach*, 2nd ed. (Kassel: Bärenreiter, 1985), vol. 2, p. 748.

11. The text is "Wenn meine Trübsal aus meine Ketten" in the *Neue Bach Ausgabe*; Professor Stauffer has kindly informed me that the manuscript has the text given above, which differs from the listings in Schmieder's catalogue. Sirp points out that the melody of the third movement aria

of Cantata 38 is derived from the opening of the chorale tune; see Sirp, "Die Thematik der Kirchenkantaten J. S. Bachs," p. 107.

12. Sirp points out that when a motive drawn from a chorale appears throughout a piece, it is usually derived from the first line of the melody; see "Die Thematik der Kirchenkantaten J. S. Bachs," p. 12. He has found only one aria in which the motivic material is drawn from each successive phrase of the chorale cantus firmus, the duet "Er kennt die rechten Freudenstunden" from Cantata 93 (Ibid., p. 17).

13. An example of this practice, known as *Vorimitationstechnik*, appears in Bach's six-voice setting of the chorale "Aus tiefer Not" in the Clavierübung III.

14. On this subject, see Charles Burkhart, "Schenker's 'Motivic Parallelisms,'" *Journal of Music Theory* 22 (1978): 145–175.

15. It seems unlikely that Bach would introduce a striking change within a ritornello without any relation to what preceded it, and there is an underlying link of a descending third between the previous sixteenth-note passage and this new passage which moves in eighth notes (see bars 16–20 in the first violin part of the ritornello). The descending third is motivically related to the initial descending third of the chorale melody. The ritornello is then rounded off by the return of the a^1–$b^{\flat 1}$–a^1–g^1–f^1 motion in bars 18–23 (example 7.6c).

16. Heinrich Schenker, "J. S. Bach: Matthauspassion, Einleitungschor (Erste Choral-Fantasie)," *Der Tonwille* 4 (1923): 3–10.

17. The opening of "Wachet auf" is very similar to that of "O Lamm Gottes." The interested reader may wish to compare the hidden enlargement shown in example 7.7 with that shown in Schenker's analysis of the opening chorus to the *St. Matthew Passion*.

18. Albert Schweitzer, *J. S. Bach*, trans. Ernest Newman (1911; reprint, New York: Dover Publications, 1966), vol. 2, pp. 247–248.

19. Sirp, "Die Thematik in Kirchenkantaten J. S. Bachs," p. 24.

20. Although bars 1–2 have no dynamic marking, they would obviously be performed *forte* so that bars 2–4 would have a typical Baroque echo effect with their *piano* dynamic. Hence there is a return to *forte* at the anacrusis to bar 5. It may be mentioned here that rising triadic figures are common in tonal music and do not necessarily have motivic meaning. In Cantata 140, the prevalence of rising triadic motives is too great to be mere coincidence; they often take on the meaning of motivic references (either on the surface or in expanded versions) to the chorale incipit.

21. There are some differences between Dürr's analysis of the famous ritornello melody and mine, as the reader can see by comparing examples 7.4 and 7.9.

Illusory Cadences and Apparent Tonics

THE EFFECT OF MOTIVIC ENLARGEMENT UPON PHRASE STRUCTURE

Eric Wen

Symmetry has long been acknowledged as an important element in the period construction of an antecedent and a consequent phrase. Although it is usual for these two phrases to be equal in length, a durational imbalance can sometimes occur between them. Leonard Ratner has stated that "classical composers were specially resourceful in building long periods by extending one or both of a pair of complementary phrases beyond their regular length by internal repetitions, interrupted cadences and harmonic digressions."[1] The inequality of phrase lengths in a period often creates a dramatic tension. In the famous duet "La ci darem," for example, Zerlina's indecision, even her reluctance, to follow Don Giovanni is descriptively portrayed by the stretching out of the consequent phrase in bars 13–18 (example 8.1). Zerlina's expanded statement of the principal theme avoids the expected final cadence in bar 16 by a motion to I^6 and a skip to $\hat{5}$ in the top voice. Not until two bars later (bar 18) does this consequent phrase reach its final cadence.

Sometimes a consequent phrase will expand specific motivic ideas presented in the antecedent. A clear example is found in the opening theme of Mozart's Quintet for piano and winds, K. 452, where the chromatic bass motion $E^\flat$–$E^\natural$–F that closes the antecedent phrase in bars 7–8 is stretched out over two extra bars in the consequent. As shown in example 8.2, instead of continuing in the same voice, the $E^\flat$ in the bass in bar 15 moves through $e^{\flat 2}$ (in the clarinet) to f^2 in bar 17. (This chromatic motive is highlighted in the right-hand part of the piano from $E^\flat$ on the second beat of bar 16 to F at the beginning of bar 17.)

Example 8.1. Mozart, "La ci darem," bars 13–18

Example 8.2. Mozart, Quintet for piano and winds, K. 452, bars 7–8 and 15–17

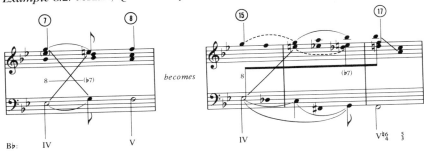

Motivic expansions can sometimes affect the tonal framework of a phrase beyond what appears to be the tonic of a final cadence. Although the closure of a consequent phrase is typically defined by an authentic cadence, tonic chords do not always signify closure. In the harmonic progression I–II⁶–"I"–V–I that supports $\hat{3}$–$\hat{2}$–$\hat{1}$–$\hat{7}$–$\hat{1}$ in the upper voice, for example, the central tonic chord functions dissimilarly from the initial and concluding tonics. It supports $\hat{1}$ as a passing tone that prolongs $\hat{2}$ by a motion into an inner voice ($\hat{2}$ = $\hat{2}$–$\hat{1}$–$\hat{7}$), and thus has no structural harmonic significance.[2] The simplicity of this example should not minimize the far-reaching consequences of such apparent tonics. Over larger spans, these "chords" can frequently be expanded into extended key areas, which do not figure structurally in the large-scale tonal framework. In the context of a development section, for example, such tonic areas can provide the tonal environment for the recollection of an opening theme, giving the impression that a reprise has begun. In a marvelous example from the first movement of Beethoven's Sixth Symphony, Heinrich Schenker shows how the tonic statement of the opening theme is brought in not to signal the beginning of the recapitulation, but to create a large-scale motivic repetition.[3] The true arrival of the recapitulation appears 10 bars later in bar 289.

This paper explores the role of apparent tonics in a specific context, elaborating several instances in Mozart's instrumental works where, due to motivic considerations, a tonic arrival in a consequent phrase does not constitute the end of a period construction. These tonics have a non-cadential function in the larger tonal framework and are only later followed by a structural tonic that closes the phrase. In these cases a motivic expansion not only extends the duration of a phrase, but also determines the structural closure of the period itself.

Piano Sonata in D, K. 576—first movement

Phrase expansion plays a significant role in the second theme of Mozart's last piano sonata. In the exposition this theme is constructed as a 12-measure period consisting of an antecedent (bars 42–45) and an extended consequent phrase (bars 46–53).[4] The consequent is not only twice the length of the antecedent, but it presents a variation of the theme embellished in sixteenth notes.

An important motive that appears throughout the movement is the descending fourth. Example 8.3 traces the various permutations of this motive within the second theme and shows its initial appearance in the sonata's opening theme. The example also illustrates that the rising fourth, C#–D–E–F#, is another motive common to both the first and second themes. Its recollection in the consequent phrase unfolds from the tonic in bar 45 to the IV chord in bar 50, as the asterisks in example 8.4 indicate.

When the second theme appears in the recapitulation (bars 122–129), it is cast as a "normal" period of equal phrase lengths. Apart from its transposition into the tonic, the antecedent is identical to its counterpart in the exposition. The consequent, however, now compresses the progression from I^6 to IV, initially unfolded in bars 48–50 of the exposition, into the first beat of bar 128. The I^6 moves immediately through IV^6 to the cadence, a motion that curtails the phrase's overall length to four bars

Example 8.3. K. 576, I, bars 42–50

Example 8.4. K. 576, I, bars 42–53

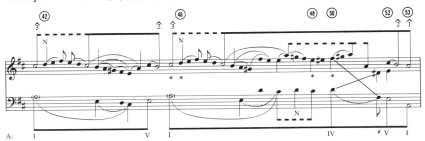

instead of eight. Another difference between the respective presentations of the second theme occurs in the top voice: both the antecedent and consequent phrases are "unembellished" in the recapitulation. The antecedent and consequent construction that occurs in bars 122–129 is thus a "normalized" version of the second theme.

Immediately following this period construction of equal phrase lengths, the second theme appears yet again (bars 130ff.). This time, however, both the antecedent and consequent phrases present the theme in its embellished form. In addition, the prolongation of the tonic in the first three bars of the antecedent (bars 130–132) is slightly recomposed: the A (V) in the bass that appears in the phrase's second bar now moves up a fourth to D (I) rather than down a third to $F^\sharp$ (I^6).

The consequent phrase of this third and final statement of the second theme is vastly expanded, and the arrival of the tonic key of D major in bar 144 is of particular interest. Beginning in bar 134, the consequent soon merges into the canonic sequence that characterizes the bridge passage in the exposition (bars 28ff.). In other words, instead of preceding the second theme as in the exposition, the canonic sequence now appears within the second theme's expanded consequent phrase. Because the conclusion of this sequence in D major (bar 144) parallels the tonicization of the dominant key area in the exposition (bar 34), this tonic would appear to have a similar structural significance (that is, the end of the consequent phrase).

Although this interpretation reveals a kind of sectional logic, an examination of the motivic threads within the second theme of the recapitulation gives a clearer picture of its structural unity. Example 8.5 presents an analytic reduction of the consequent phrase and shows how the two bars immediately preceding the sequential passage initiate a large-scale statement of the motive of a descending fourth. The top line over bars 136–137, a^2–$g^{\sharp 2}$–$g^{\natural 2}$–$f^{\sharp 2}$, continues 15 bars later (bar 152) with $f^{\natural 3}$ supported by a diminished seventh chord on $G^\sharp$. The $f^{\natural 3}$ resolves to e^2 over the dominant chord in bar 154 and is especially significant because it is the

Example 8.5. K. 576, I, bars 134–155

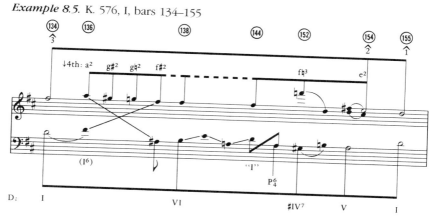

highest note of the entire movement.[5] Furthermore, bars 153–160 are an exact transposition of the end of the exposition (bars 51–58), meaning that the consequent phrase extends past the D-major episode in bars 144ff. until the final cadence in bar 155.[6] As shown in example 8.5, the tonic in bar 144 does not signal the end of the consequent phrase, but represents an unfolding of a passing six-four chord connecting VI in bar 138 with ♯IV[7] in bar 152.[7]

Symphony in E♭, K. 543—fourth movement

Although it is commonly noted that the Finale of Mozart's Symphony no. 39 is a monothematic sonata form, the first and second presentations of the theme (in the tonic and dominant key areas) are presented in completely different ways: the second theme recalls the opening melodic idea but is cast in an antecedent-consequent construction. Example 8.6 illustrates the tonal structure of the second theme's antecedent phrase.

What is particularly distinctive about the second theme's consequent phrase is its unusual enharmonic passage and its extended final cadence.

Example 8.6. K. 543, IV, bars 42–47

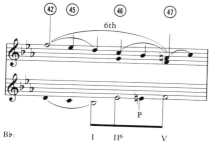

The consequent phrase begins exactly like the antecedent, but alters the tonic key of B♭ major to its parallel minor in bar 50. The II⁶ following the opening four-measure prolongation of the tonic is also affected by the modal mixture to minor and is cast as a Phrygian II. For notational convenience this chord is enharmonically notated as B major instead of C♭ major.

Example 8.7 presents a chordal reduction of the opening segment in the consequent's expansion (the Phrygian II is shown here as C♭), and shows how the Phrygian II leads to the dominant six-five that reestablishes tonic harmony in bar 66. The bass motion is articulated into two descending thirds: E♭(D♯)–C♯ and C♮–A♮. A diminished seventh chord serves as the midpoint of these two linear progressions in the bass and functions as a pivot for the enharmonic transformation that occurs over these bars.

The B♭ cadence in bars 66–68 brings tonal stability to the phrase and would appear to articulate the end of the consequent. Example 8.8 shows, however, that this locally expanded tonic has an altogether different function. Rather than closing the consequent phrase, the tonic chord in bar 68 serves as the midpoint of an arpeggiation leading from the Phrygian II in bar 52 to the augmented sixth chord in bar 73, and it anticipates the B♭ of the augmented sixth. The E♮ in the top voice of the augmented sixth chord, which leads directly to F in the dominant of bars 74–79, derives from a chromatic inflection through a voice exchange of the E♭ in the ♭II⁶ in bar 52. This chromatic line—E♭–E♮–F—unifies the entire phrase and is an expanded repetition of the chromatic bass motion in bars 46–47 (second violin) of the antecedent.

The brief passage that concludes the consequent phrase begins in bar 79 and expands the rising third A–C, which initially appeared in the top voice at the end of the antecedent (bar 47), over three measures (see the first violin part in bars 79–81). Moreover, this passage initiates the structural descent from $\hat{5}$, first stated in bar 48. Example 8.9 shows that $\hat{5}$ to $\hat{4}$ results from an 8–7 motion over the dominant in bars 79–82 (the C-minor chord in bar 81 prepares $\hat{4}$), a motion highlighted by the top notes of

Example 8.7. K. 543, IV, bars 52–66

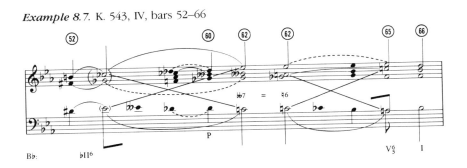

Example 8.8. K. 543, IV, bars 48–79

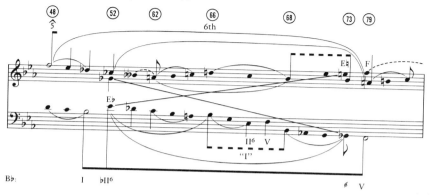

Example 8.9. K. 543, IV, bars 79–85

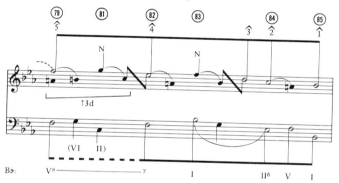

the descending fifths in the clarinet (bars 80 and 82). The remainder of the fundamental line unfolds over a complete harmonic progression; as a result, the consequent phrase, as shown in examples 8.8 and 8.9, is articulated over bars 48–85 by a large-scale, double harmonic progression.

Piano Concerto in B♭, K. 595—first movement

The final phrase expansion to be discussed occurs at the end of the orchestral ritornello in Mozart's Piano Concerto in B♭,[8] where the repetition of the closing gesture produces an antecedent-consequent relationship of phrases (bars 47ff.).[9] Example 8.10 presents a reduction of the initial phrase and shows that a chromatic inflection of E♭ to E♮ appears in the voice exchange of bars 47–48. This alteration transforms the IV⁶ on the second beat of bar 47 into a diminished seventh chord that functions as a ♮IV♭⁷; conceptually, this foreground transformation simply represents 8–♭7 over IV leading to the dominant of the phrase.[10]

Example 8.10. K. 595, I, bars 47–50

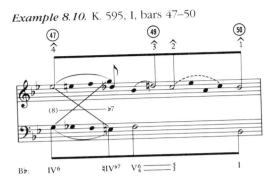

Beginning in bar 50, the consequent phrase opens similarly to the antecedent phrase with a voice exchange in which one of the voices is chromatically altered. Instead of chromatically raising E♭ to E♮, however, this voice exchange chromatically inflects G in the bass to G♭ in the top voice. This is a subtle but significant change from the parallel place in the antecedent, because the resultant diminished seventh chord in bar 51 now functions as a VII⁴₃ that resolves into the minor form of a first-inversion tonic chord. As shown in example 8.11, the B♭-minor chord on the last beat of bar 51 does not represent a return to the tonic, but serves as a passing chord between the opening IV⁶ and the ♭II⁶ in bar 52. Mozart's use of the Phrygian II underscores the context of B♭ minor (bars 51–54) that provides an especially poignant contrast of mode before B♭ major returns in bar 55.[11]

A significant feature of the B♭-major chord in bar 55 is that it contains the lowered seventh, A♭. This tonicizes the subdominant chord at the beginning of bar 56 and has the effect of extending the phrase. Although an authentic cadence in B♭ follows, the upper neighbor E♭ (4̂) of the IV chord extends beyond the V in bar 57 and resolves to D only in bar 59 (example

Example 8.11. K. 595, I, bars 50–55

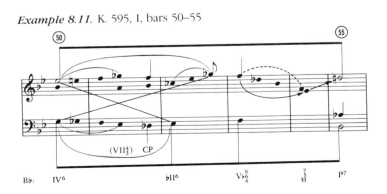

8.12).[12] Despite the reiteration of this cadence in bars 60–64, the consequent phrase remains "in progress" because D is prolonged and remains the main tone in the upper voice.

Example 8.13 presents an analytic sketch of the entire consequent phrase and shows how the expansion of B♭-major harmony (bars 55–64) has a subordinate function within the larger harmonic motion of the phrase. The structural V does not appear until bar 68, and the phrase finally closes with the arrival of the tonic in the following bar. What is significant in this final cadence is that the diminished seventh chord immediately preceding the structural V in bar 68 represents a ♮IV♭⁷ that relates to the IV⁶ chord at the opening of the phrase. This connection reveals that the basic progression of bars 50–67 is an expanded statement of IV⁶–♮IV♭⁷, initially stated in the first two bars of the antecedent phrase (example 8.10). The D that is supported by the expansion of B♭ harmony is not part of the fundamental melodic line, but is a chromatic passing tone between E♭ and

Example 8.12. K. 595, I, bars 55–64

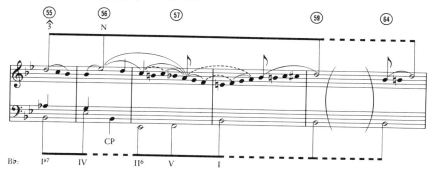

Example 8.13. K. 595, I, bars 50–69

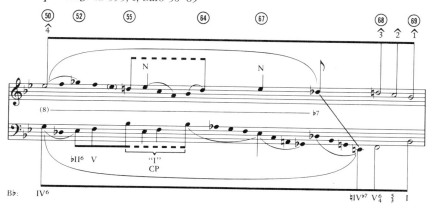

D♭ over IV. The earlier digression into B♭ minor in bar 51 not only provides a poignant contrast of mode at the opening of the phrase, but foreshadows the D♭ that ultimately completes the 8–♭7 motion over the subdominant harmony prolonged in bars 50–67.

Although it has been noted that the end of an exposition contains a number of cadences that reiterate its closure through the expression of the second theme's tonic harmony,[13] it is clear from the examples discussed above, all of which are subordinate themes in sonata movements, that some of these cadences (and corresponding tonics) can serve a nonstructural function within the larger tonal progression of a single theme. The recurrence of tonic harmony within a theme thus does not necessarily signal its closure, but can have a variety of meanings depending upon the motivic threads that may unify the theme as a whole.

NOTES

1. Leonard Ratner, "Period," *The New Grove Dictionary of Music and Musicians*, ed. Stanley Sadie (London: Macmillan, 1980), vol. 14, p. 407.
2. Larry Laskowski discusses this particular tonal progression in his article "Context and Voice Leading: Influences on Thematic and Tonal Structure," *Theory and Practice*, 4, 2 (March 1979): 15–24.
3. See Schenker's graphic analysis of bars 275ff. from the first movement of Beethoven's Sixth Symphony in *Free Composition*, trans. and ed. Ernst Oster (New York: Schirmer Books, 1979), fig. 119,8.
4. William Caplin discusses this theme in his article "The 'Expanded Cadential Progression': A Category for the Analysis of Form," *Journal of Musicological Research*, 7 (1987): 222–227. He calls bars 42ff. the "second" subordinate theme of the exposition and refers to bars 28ff. as the "first" subordinate theme. Although the arrival in the dominant is made before this "first" subordinate theme, the invention-like nature of the passage in bars 28ff. is more suggestive of a transitional section than a proper theme.
5. The F♯ has a further significance as the enharmonic equivalent of E♯ that appeared in the second half of bar 49. The two enharmonic forms of the same note appear in expansions of the second theme's consequent phrase in both the exposition and recapitulation.
6. It is also worth noting that bar 132 is similar in rhythm and gesture to bar 50.
7. Another remarkable example of an apparent tonic is found in Bach's B♭-minor Fugue (WTC I). The stretto passage in bars 67ff. forms part

of a similar unfolding of a passing six-four chord between a IV^6 in bar 64 and a ♮IV^7 in bar 73.

8. For the purposes of this article, I have used the Dover reprint of Breitkopf & Härtel's complete works edition (New York: Dover Publications, 1978). The *Neue Ausgabe sämtlicher Werke* (Kassel: Bärenreiter, 1960) shows seven bars that are not in the earlier edition; since they do not pertain to my discussion, I have used the more accessible version.

9. The relationship of antecedent and consequent phrases is not restricted to the tonal scheme whereby the antecedent states an incomplete harmonic progression that is restated and resolved in the consequent. Two complementary phrases that articulate the same harmonic progression can also be regraded as an antecedent-consequent construction. Schenker describes bars 5–8 and bars 9–11 of the first movement of Mozart's Sonata in C, K. 330, as antecedent and consequent phrases, and remarks that the former "gives satisfaction of a preliminary, relative kind" whereas the latter "brings the final and absolute satisfaction of a concluded thought." See Schenker, *Harmony*, ed. Oswald Jonas, trans. Elisabeth Mann Borgese (Chicago: University of Chicago Press, 1954 and 1980), p. 216. In his extensive analysis of Mozart's Symphony no. 40 in G minor, Schenker describes the two phrases that make up the second theme of the first movement, both of which cadence in the tonic, as being in an antecedent-consequent relationship. See Schenker, *Das Meisterwerk in der Musik* (3 vols.; Munich: Drei Masken Verlag, 1925, 1926, 1930 [reissued as 3 vols. in 1 slightly reduced facsimile, Hildesheim: Olms, 1974]), vol. 2, pp. 113–114.

10. The motion from G to E in the bass of bars 47–48 echoes the skip in the bass from VI to ♮IV^7 in bars 31 and 35, as well as bar 11 of the opening theme itself.

11. The C♭ arpeggio over the Phrygian II in bar 52 echoes the very opening theme of the concerto. Furthermore, it enharmonically prepares the opening theme's remarkable transposition into B minor at the beginning of the development section (bars 184ff.).

12. This delayed resolution of $\hat{4}$ to $\hat{3}$ appears earlier in bars 38–40. The seventh of the V^7 (e♭^{2}) in bar 38 does not resolve to d^2 until bar 40.

13. "At the end of the exposition, in order to confirm the new harmonic center, a considerable amount of insistence upon the now-tonicized dominant is called for. At this point, the most conventional material is often found with cadential phrases repeated many times over." See Charles Rosen, *Sonata Forms*, 2nd ed. (W. W. Norton: New York, 1988), p. 242.

Handel's Borrowings from Telemann

AN ANALYTICAL VIEW

Channan Willner

Of the major issues that Handel scholars have had to confront through the years, few have proved as problematic—or as fascinating—as Handel's dependence on the music of other composers for thematic ideas, melodic invention, and other compositional resources.[1] During the Handel tercentenary celebrations of 1985, the study of Handel borrowings was reinvested with new life: John Roberts launched the publication of a facsimile edition of vocal and operatic sources for Handel's borrowings, many unearthed and newly added to the canon by Roberts himself.[2] Moreover, Ellwood Derr and Roberts published two major studies and an inventory of Handel's borrowings from Telemann's *Harmonischer Gottes-Dienst, Musique de table*, and *Sonates sans basse*.[3] As Derr and Roberts have most convincingly shown, Handel's borrowings vary enormously in type, scope, content, and purpose; they must be examined within the larger framework of the compositions in which they occur for their full significance and meaning to emerge.

In this study I compare two Handel concerto movements and an oratorio "symphony" with the concerto and overture movements from Telemann's *Musique de table* on which they are based. I address the compositional implications of the rhythmic, motivic, stylistic, and tonal similarities and differences between the corresponding movements. Among other things, I show how these surface features and broader relationships may point, each in its own way, to patterns and criteria in Handel's use of Telemann's source materials. This in turn reveals how we may define and account for the scope of Handel's reliance on Telemann's music, and helps us to evaluate the true extent of Handel's fidelity to Telemann's text.

Before turning to our three principal examples, I should like to discuss briefly a relatively straightforward appropriation that throws into relief one of Handel's most important borrowing techniques, namely, that of recomposition. Understanding Handel's mastery of recomposition is central to any investigation of his borrowings and is of special importance to our investigation of the first and third borrowings under discussion. In contrast to borrowings that are essentially literal or to those where the original material becomes very deeply hidden under the surface, recomposition as viewed here involves substantial alteration of the surface without fundamental changes to its essential motivic or structural kernel. This is a procedure to which Handel subjects his *own* material time and again, often to an extent that far transcends the familiar notion of self-borrowing: passages introduced earlier in the course of a piece frequently tend to reappear, transmogrified, carrying out some new thematic or contrapuntal task (see example 9.1, which shows a recomposition from the Allemande of the D-minor keyboard Suite of 1720).[4] Recompositions of this sort represent one of the most sophisticated and rarefied of Handel's compositional procedures: in employing recomposition as a means of reworking other composers' music, Handel elevated the art of borrowing to an entirely new, and eminently creative, artistic plane.[5]

Our example of straightforward appropriation (often cited in the scholarly literature but examined here from a new perspective) involves the expansive opening of Handel's Organ Concerto in B♭, op. 7, no. 6 (example 9.2b),[6] which is a wide-spanning but readily detectable recomposition of the gradually rising arpeggiation in the opening bars of Telemann's Concerto in E♭ for two natural horns from *Musique de table* (example 9.2a).[7] Telemann's arpeggiation traverses several rising sixths that are separated by essentially identical, complementary falling sixths (see the brackets in example 9.2a). Despite the embellishing addition of Scotch snaps, the upward sweep of the rising sixths is compromised through both their subsequent descending repetition and the anticipation

Example 9.1. Handel, Suite in D minor (1720, HWV 428), Allemande

becomes

of the arpeggiation's tones by the Scotch snaps. Upon taking over the rising and falling sixths, Handel not only reverses their direction (turning one into a fifth in the process) but, more important, adds several pivotal changes in direction (see the arrows in example 9.2b). He also assigns each sixth an independent and distinct tonal space; this allows the sixths to open up and introduce higher registral areas and thus expand greatly both the tonal space they traverse individually and the ambitus embraced by the opening theme as a whole. The theme consequently ascends much more steeply than Telemann's and does so in a sweeping gesture, allowing Telemann's somewhat constricted tune to break free of its relatively rigid intervallic shackles.[8]

The more elaborate borrowings we are about to discuss are not only more complex, involving as they do questions of harmonic rhythm, large-scale structure, and style: two of the three borrowings show far more extensive changes in the surface of Telemann's original material than did the example just given. Common to all three, however, is the opportunity their use of recomposition affords us to visit the inner chambers of Han-

Example 9.2a. Telemann, *Musique de table*, Concerto for two natural horns, I, opening theme

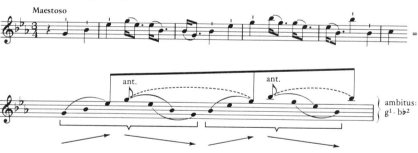

Example 9.2b. Handel, Organ Concerto, op. 7, no. 6 (HWV 311), I, opening theme

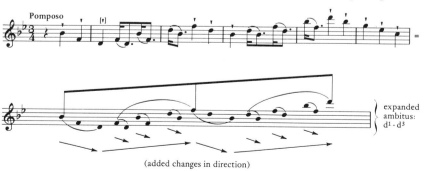

(added changes in direction)

del's workshop, and to observe some of his working methods from very close range.

I should like to emphasize at the outset that it is inevitable for any comparison between related works of Handel and Telemann to stress Handel's resourcefulness at the expense of Telemann's compositional expertise. This of necessity does Telemann something of a disservice and an injustice, for much of his music was composed under musical and social circumstances different from Handel's and was molded by different compositional aims. An analytical study of Telemann's music on its own terms, independent of comparisons as a frame of reference, reveals many fine and well-crafted works whose value has only recently begun to be appreciated and understood by performing musicians, the listening public, and the musicological community.[9]

I

The first-movement ritornello of Handel's popular Concerto Grosso in C, known as the "Concerto in Alexander's Feast,"[10] clearly derives from the Finale ritornello of the Concerto in A for flute, violin, cello, and strings from part I of Telemann's *Musique de table*;[11] one might legitimately even consider it a free paraphrase of its source (examples 9.3a and 9.3b).[12] The tripartite design of both ritornelli is substantially similar, despite differences in rhythmic grouping and in the length of cadential extensions;[13] and some permutation notwithstanding, the derivation of Handel's thematic material from Telemann's ritornello is quite obvious (Table 9.1).[14]

As the reductions in example 9.4 show, Handel's ritornello is fundamentally far more mobile than Telemann's, rising and falling in carefully balanced, complementary linear motions and steps. Telemann's ritornello not only is much more stationary and narrow in ambitus, it does not connect the essential tones of the middle section (bars 7–10), not even the leading tone $g^{\sharp 2}$, to anything in the preceding or following section (it

Table 9.1
Derivation of Handel's Thematic and Harmonic Material from Telemann's Concerto

	A	B	C
Handel	bars 1–4		
	based	bars 5–8	bars 9–18
	on	based on	based on
Telemann	bars 1–4	bars 7–10	bars 7–10
		(harmonically)	(melodically and harmonically)
			and on bars 15, 21

Example 9.3a. Handel, "Concerto in Alexander's Feast" (HWV 318), I, ritornello

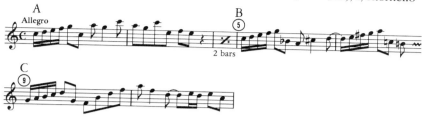

Example 9.3b. Telemann, *Musique de table*, Concerto for flute, violin, and cello, IV, ritornello

does, however, include several ingeniously varied restatements and enlargements of the descending step motive marked by brackets in example 9.4b). As for the details of Handel's recomposition, one might single out the stability and steadiness of the melodic line in bars 1–2, which lingers much longer on $\hat{5}$ and thus contrasts sharply with Telemann's tentative emphasis on the same scale degree and his much more disjunct melodic line. And although Handel incorporates Telemann's opening run of a fifth as a surface motive at the beginning of each measure of his middle section (bars 5–8), he also recomposes it at a higher artistic level: the fifth unfolds over the span of the entire section.[15]

An important similarity between the two movements lies in the design of the solo-tutti exchanges: the motivic working-out of the solo parts throughout both movements is interrupted at more or less regular intervals by fragmented quotations of the ritornello that, step by step, describe the ritornello over an extended span of time (see Handel, bars 23–24, 31–32, and similar passages; Telemann, bars 28–29, 33–34, 63–64, etc.). This device helps keep both movements taut (essential in the rather loosely constructed Telemann), and the contrasts in textural and thematic design it fosters lend both movements a propulsive rhythmic impetus.

As it happens, however, the differences between the two movements in this instance outweigh the similarities, and are well worth investigating

Example 9.4a. Handel, "Concerto in Alexander's Feast," ritornello, tonal and rhythmic outline

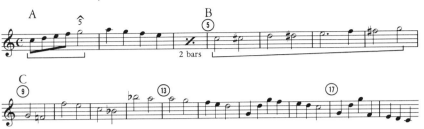

Example 9.4b. Telemann, Concerto, ritornello, tonal and rhythmic outline

further. By and large, Handel's harmonic rhythm at the foreground is distinctly faster than Telemann's, comprising as it does, in typically Baroque fashion, two or (more often) four harmonies in each bar (example 9.5a). Telemann's, on the other hand, despite obvious accelerations, often consists essentially of one harmony per bar, and thus foreshadows the harmonic rhythm of the later Classical and pre-Classical styles (example 9.5b).[16]

A corresponding difference also obtains in the two composers' motivic treatment. Handel employs typically Baroque spinning-out and sequential elaboration, at times seemingly independent of the ritornello but often reflecting its outlines in many ways and on many levels (example 9.6a; note how the ritornello's syncopation figures are seamlessly varied in the solo sections, as shown in example 9.6b). Telemann, by contrast, builds on highly neutral—and, in a sense, abstract—thematic cells that show, at best, only tenuous relation to the ritornello or to each other (example 9.7). Thus the thematic tension in Handel's Concerto is generated through a highly improvisatory yet tightly controlled succession of motivic events; it has no real counterpart, let alone origin or basis, in Telemann's movement. The tension in Telemann's Concerto, such as it exists, results not

Example 9.5a. Handel, "Concerto in Alexander's Feast," second solo entrance, harmonic rhythm

Example 9.5b. Telemann, Concerto, first soli entrance, harmonic rhythm

Example 9.6a. Handel, "Concerto in Alexander's Feast," motivic treatment

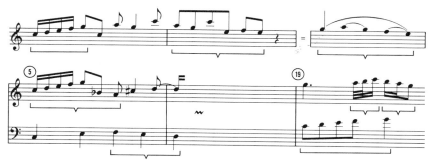

Example 9.6b. Rhythmic treatment

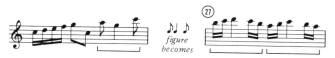

Example 9.7. Telemann, Concerto, motivic treatment

from motivic and rhythmic development in Baroque style as we know it, but from the contrast and opposition among the larger thematic groups and from the difficulty of predicting the contents of each successive group (qualities that, incidentally, also account for much of the charm of his composition).[17]

The relation between solo and tutti is far more systematically worked out by Handel than by Telemann. Handel's tutti, even when reaching beyond the immediate domain of the tonic, retain an essential link with the scale degrees that outline the tonic's tonal space between C and G (example 9.8a); the solo writing, on the other hand, even during surface prolongations of the tonic, revolves around the scale degrees of the dominant and the tonal space between G and B or B♭, a feature underscored in striking fashion at the solo instruments' first entrance (as the brackets in examples 9.8b–8d show, Handel's effortless resourcefulness in varying the tone successions B–A–G and G–A–B *in different tonal contexts* at each appearance is most remarkable). The solo sections can therefore be interpreted as free, if more or less hidden, variants (or developing variations) of each other: the internal relationship unites the three solo instruments in their proverbial conflict with the tutti.[18]

No comparable relationships between soli and tutti, or even among the solo sections, can be found in Telemann's concerto movement—at least none that I could detect. The contrast between the two concerto movements can be discerned in the design of their underlying structures: the larger outlines of Handel's movement are far more complex and elab-

Example 9.8a. Handel, "Concerto in Alexander's Feast," bass motion outline

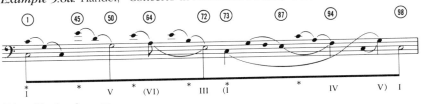

*Ritornelli and tutti passages

Example 9.8b. Tonal space in solo passages, I–V

Example 9.8c. Tonal space, V–VI

Example 9.8d. Tonal space, VI–III

orately worked out than those of Telemann's. As example 9.8a shows, the central tonicization of the dominant in Handel is followed by a very gradual return to the tonic through brief tonicizations of the submediant and mediant, and through an auxiliary cadence that anticipates the tonic at the surface and supports a token recapitulation (the tonic emerges as a higher-order scale step only at the conclusion of the movement). In Telemann, the larger voice leading reaches only for the subdominant and the dominant before settling on an extended reprise, in which the function of the tonic is not designated or established with any degree of clarity (example 9.9). Telemann's simple tonal plan and its blunt execution, much like his unsystematic motivic treatment, looks forward, if that is the right word, to the uncomplicated, trouble-free world of the mid-century symphonists; Handel's intricately joined succession of keys belongs, by contrast, to the more complex world of the Baroque.

Despite the similarities resulting from Handel's borrowing, then, the two composers' approaches are quite different. In borrowing motivic fragments, thematic units, and even larger entities from Telemann, Handel seems to have chosen here mainly those "retrogressive" elements that most closely fitted his own cosmopolitan but conservative style; he evidently rejected many of the more "progressive" aspects of Telemann's music. The Telemann materials he did incorporate he translated into his

Example 9.9. Telemann, Concerto, bass motion outline

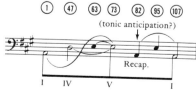

own inimitable language, and with such success that in most instances one's attention is hardly drawn to the borrowings as such, even if one knows their origins and is keenly aware of their presence.[19]

II

In the second movement from the Organ Concerto in D minor/major, op. 7, no. 4 (example 9.10),[20] Handel's borrowing—from the ritornello of the Air from the Overture in D for oboe, trumpet, and strings, *Musique de table*, part II (example 9.11)[21]—is much more literal; indeed, it often seems to take over Telemann's model and follow it almost note for note.[22] And Handel's movement, as such, is only skeletal in outline: much of the solo

Example 9.10. Handel, Organ Concerto, op. 7, no. 4 (HWV 309), II, ritornello

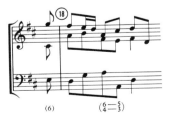

Example 9.11. Telemann, *Musique de table*, Air, ritornello

passagework is left for the soloist to improvise *ad libitum*. There would therefore naturally seem to be more Telemann than Handel here, yet when approached from a larger—even slightly larger—thematic, tonal, and rhythmic perspective, Handel's deceptively modest changes and additions take on great significance. It is, in fact, their very moderation that underscores their far-reaching extent and helps reconfirm Handel's great resourcefulness and originality in reworking source material.

As it happens, Telemann's Air is much more characteristically Baroque than his concerto movement we have just discussed: its harmonic rhythm is faster, and its motivic groups are both shorter and more clearly defined. Nonetheless, like Handel's seeming adherence to Telemann's text, the greater stylistic similarity between source and borrowing in this instance only underlines the fundamental differences between the two.

Unlike our earlier Handel ritornello, which was shorter and more concise than Telemann's prototype, Handel's ritornello here is more extended. The solo organ, rather than the orchestra, enters first, with a two-measure anticipation of the orchestral entrance; a two-measure interpolation of the tonic in first inversion is added in bars 11 and 12, after the arrival on the subdominant in bar 10; and the closing tonic extends over four, rather than two, measures (bars 15–18).[23] To understand the meaning of these additions, we must compare the two composers' approach to large-scale rhythm. Telemann repeats bars 3 and 4, instead of introducing a new two-measure group, in bars 5 and 6. Although the repetition, superficially, seems to work, its appearance so early in the movement introduces a sense of four-measure grouping that conflicts with the prevailing context of two-measure groups. While Telemann does not grapple with this problem at all, Handel provides the rhythmic enlargement with both preparation—the added organ entrance—and the two follow-up additions we have just observed, thereby retaining Telemann's two-measure groups but organizing them within a clearer framework of four plus four.

Now as a result of the tonic interpolation in Handel's ritornello (bars 11–12), the preceding subdominant, which remains the underlying harmony, becomes substantially expanded (example 9.12). This expansion engenders a parallelism between the bass motion in bars 1–2 and 1–8 on the one hand, and the ritornello's long-span bass progression on the other; it also allows Handel to expand the earlier sequential descent from a^2 in the upper voice (see the asterisks and brackets throughout examples 9.10 and 9.12). On a level closer to the foreground, Handel's treatment of the bass note G in bars 1–2—a spot often chosen by the great composers for the introduction of material earmarked for later elaboration at various levels—represents a tonal counterpart to the rhythmic two-measure additions; it is, in fact, a feature of some complexity and requires detailed examination.

At the opening of Telemann's Air (example 9.11), a pungent if slightly ungainly motion from B to G, which is marked by a weak and premature statement of G early in bar 1, is followed by an ambiguous alternation between F♯ and G in the bass (see the two brackets in example 9.11). In Handel's Concerto, the bass G appears only after the upper-voice arpeggiation, which replaces Telemann's repeated D's, has been completed, and its entrance is lent emphasis by a dramatic new element—an eighth-note caesura rest which abruptly halts the music in mid-phrase, at the II^6 chord that G supports (example 9.10). As a result of its highly exposed introduction, the treatment of G in the bass throughout the movement (both as neighbor of F♯ and as a passing tone on the way to A) becomes a compositional issue of potential importance—and its importance is im-

Example 9.12. Handel, Organ Concerto, ritornello, middleground sketch.

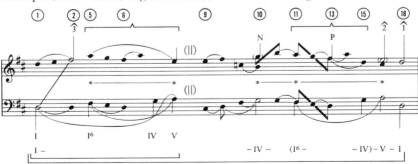

mediately confirmed by the ensuing alternation with F♯, which centers unequivocally on G and thus clarifies its purpose more readily than in Telemann's ritornello. Telemann, in fact, makes no effort to capitalize on the manifold possibilities of his colorful progression: in the course of his ritornello he touches on G only twice more, briefly, in bars 8 and 12, and not at all during the repeated approach to the dividing dominant in bars 4 and 6 (example 9.13). Note especially how minor is the role played by Telemann's first-inversion tonic after the opening measure: Handel's tonic, by contrast (in conjunction with the expanded G), becomes the basis for a hidden repetition and expansion of bars 5–8 in bars 11–15 (see the asterisks in example 9.12).

The foursquare simplicity of Telemann's larger harmonic planning, especially its exclusion of substantially worked-out intermediate harmonies between the tonic and the dominant, again represents stark premonition of the simpler harmonic framework of the pre-Classical style. And it is no coincidence that Telemann's foreground is replete with harmonically directed root-position chords. Handel, then, did not merely elaborate on Telemann's model: he replanted its essentially Galant harmonic framework in the more contrapuntal ground of the Baroque.

A most important stylistic and compositional difference between the Handel and Telemann works, one that affects their thematic design at every turn, lies in the two composers' fundamentally different approaches to motivic design and its rhythmic implications. Among the most conspicuous figures that Telemann culls from his ritornello for developmental fragmentation in the solo sections (his material here lending itself more readily to development than the concerto movement discussed earlier) are a characteristic repeated falling-arpeggio motive (example 9.14a) and a rapid repeated descending-third upbeat figure (example 9.14b). Now in both composers' ritornelli each series of repeated falling-arpeggio motives and descending-third figures functions as a prefix to a new motivic and rhythmic group (the square brackets in example 9.14 show the approach to each new group; the curly brackets, the new group itself). As the solo

Example 9.13. Telemann, Air, ritornello, middleground sketch

part of Handel's Concerto unfolds, the series of falling-arpeggio motives and descending-third figures retain their function as prefixes to new groups that are similar to those in the ritornello: the larger rhythmic meaning of the motives and figures remains unchanged, in keeping with the consistency of motivic treatment that was characteristic of the high Baroque (example 9.15).

In Telemann's Air, on the other hand, both the series of falling-arpeggio motives and the descending-third figures often do change their rhythmic meaning within the larger thematic context from prefix to suffix (and the change is quite startling in performance). The reason for their transformation is that they are made to perform double duty as developmental solo figures and as neutrally accompanimental turns of phrase; the new groups to which they lead are often in no way comparable to those found in the ritornello. In some instances, in fact, they relinquish their role as prefixes to new groups altogether (see example 9.16: the curly brackets indicate Telemann's modification or abandonment of the new groups). More often than not the restatement of each series of falling-arpeggio motives and descending-third figures coincides with a downbeat very much like that which, in introducing a new group, the motives and figures *preceded* and helped prepare in the ritornello. And Telemann's principal developmental figure (which Handel hardly employs in this capacity) is the rather unlikely closing figure of his ritornello (example 9.16c). Employing such a closing figure for the purpose of development was to become standard practice in the later Classical period, but within Telemann's temporally more restricted framework the procedure is awkward: a conceptually weak rhythmic figure (with a distinct formal function of its own) is associated with stronger rhythmic implications and an entirely different formal purpose.

Telemann's apparent willingness to compromise the rhythmic and formal essence of his basic material while working it out is again emblematic of the gradual breakdown of motivic and rhythmic procedures

Example 9.14. Telemann, Air, rhythmic relations in ritornello

Example 9.15. Handel, Organ Concerto, rhythmic relations in solo sections

Example 9.16. Telemann, Air, rhythmic relations in solo sections

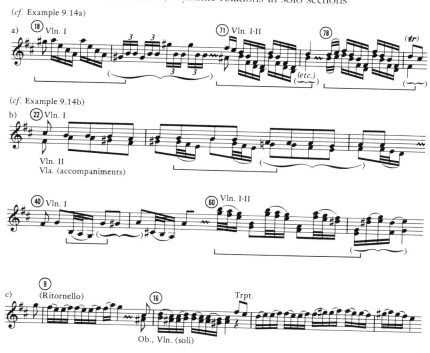

that was beginning to take place across the Continent; motivic and thematic consistency was, if temporarily, about to lose its status as a compositional requirement or ideal.[24] It should come as no surprise, then, that Handel, the quintessential Baroque composer, would take over only Telemann's ritornello, which presents concise expository material that had remained largely untapped by its composer, and would make virtually no use of the ambivalent thematic and rhythmic discourse of Telemann's solo sections.

In what concerns Handel's apparently literal adoption of Telemann's ritornello melody, one is again struck by the expansion and more wide-ranging use of the effective ambitus of the melodic line (from d^1–d^3 to g–d^3): the theme now emerges and rises from the one-line to the two-line octave (bars 1, 3, 9–10 and 15–16) and, as a concluding flourish, reestablishes the tonal space of the three-line octave touched upon in bars 11 and 12. In the first two bars, to single out one important and conspicuous result of this spatial enlargement, the widened range allows Handel to change Telemann's melodically neutral prefixes (example 9.17a) into highly directed upbeats (example 9.17b) and to do away altogether with Telemann's insistent repetition of the eighth note d^2; as a result, Handel

Example 9.17a. Telemann, Air, opening bars, sketch

Example 9.17b. Handel, Organ Concerto, opening bars, sketch

can reduce the rhythmic activity at the turn of bar 4 and gain a far more shapely melodic line.

III

In our first pair of Handel and Telemann compositions we saw Handel use Telemann's ritornello as a free thematic, textural, and formal basis for a highly original composition; in our second pair we found him realizing the tonal and rhythmic possibilities inherent in Telemann's model without making extensive changes in it. Our third and final pair embodies the hallmarks of both these borrowings and at the same time incorporates a major borrowing from a second composer, Giovanni Porta.

The Symphony that opens the third act of Handel's oratorio, *Solomon*, better known as the "Arrival of the Queen of Sheba" (example 9.18a),[25] represents a hybrid borrowing: its ritornello derives from the opening of the Concerto in F for three violins and strings from part II of *Musique de table* (example 9.18b),[26] while its beguiling oboe-duet exchanges are based on an aria from Porta's opera, *Numitore* (compare examples 9.19a and 9.19b); Handel also had previously used much the same material from *Numitore* in the fourth movement of the Overture in C for two clarinets and horn (example 9.19c).[27] Because Handel's solo writing here is entirely unrelated to Telemann's, a look at the long-range design and underlying structure that support the borrowing and its intimate links to the material borrowed from Porta's Aria and the Overture for two clarinets will prove more fruitful than a detailed comparison of foreground relationships. This will in turn allow us to apprehend the meaning of the new mold in which Handel casts Telemann's ritornello.

Handel alters the surface of Telemann's ritornello in several important ways (only some of these are illustrated in examples 9.18 and 9.19, but all are significant for the design of Handel's recomposition): he recomposes the surface configuration of Telemann's characteristic rising sixteenth note arpeggio figures so that they fall before the deeper melodic

Example 9.18a. Handel, *Solomon,* "Arrival of the Queen of Sheba," ritornello

Example 9.18b. Telemann, *Musique de table,* Concerto for three violins, I, ritornello

Example 9.19a. Handel, "Queen of Sheba," oboe exchanges

Example 9.19b. Porta, *Numitore,* "Sol m'affanna," introduction

Example 9.19c. Handel, Overture for two clarinets and horn (HWV 424), IV

line they describe begins to rise (see the arrows and asterisks in examples 9.18a and 9.18b—Handel's extensive changes in direction, especially the displacement of the first melody tone in bar 2, are of particular significance); he reroutes the voice leading to the dominant in bars 3–4, adding a two-measure retransition to the tonic in bars 5–6; he dispenses entirely with Telemann's middle section (bars 10–13); and instead of incorporating Telemann's Italianate but awkward modal mixture, he derives more ef-

Example 9.20. Handel, "Queen of Sheba," sketches

fective tonal contrast from the diatonic minor harmonies II and VI through which he repeatedly passes.

Handel's most far-reaching alterations and recompositions, though, appear at a deeper level, through the projection of a melodic kernel from the surface of Porta's Aria into the structural framework of the entire Symphony. This enlargement is accomplished by the gradual expansion of the harmonic region governed by E♭ in the bass, which initially appears as part of a I–II⁶–V–I progression in bars 1–2 (example 9.20a). The same progression subsequently spans the entire ritornello, where the supertonic is extended by a voice exchange between II and II⁶ (example 9.20b). Over a longer span and at a still deeper level, E♭ supports the enlargement and transformation of IV into II⁶₅ by a 5–6 motion before the structural dominant enters in bar 79 (example 9.20c).

It is these essential tonal expansions that support a series of enlargements in the long-span melodic motion of the upper voice. A pair of underlying third-progressions $\hat{3}$–$\hat{2}$–$\hat{1}$, from d² to b♭¹, support both the ritornello and the Symphony as a whole; the primary tone ($\hat{3}$) of each is embellished and prolonged through the expanded, recomposed repetition of a motive that permeates the surface of Porta's Aria, namely, the succession of tones d²–f²–e♭²–d² (compare examples 9.20b and 9.20c with the beginning of Handel's Overture in example 9.19c and with the beginning of Porta's Aria in example 9.19b; the square brackets throughout examples 9.19 and 9.20 show the contour of this fundamental tone succession). These motivic relationships are manifest at every level in Handel's Symphony, for at the surface Handel again employs the same melodic kernel as the thematic basis for the Symphony's oboe exchanges (example 9.19a). Thus in fashioning his own Symphony, Handel implants Porta's most characteristic melodic progression at several different levels under the surface of his recomposition of Telemann's ritornello.[28]

In the course of this study, I have attempted to demonstrate that Handel's mastery as a composer, in and of itself, owes little to the sources of his

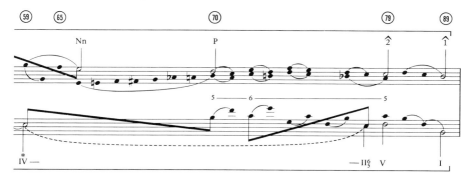

borrowings. At least in the examples presented here, Handel employs Telemann's materials on a highly selective and conservative basis, retaining complete compositional autonomy and preventing the borrowings from assuming any degree of control over his music.

That Handel's borrowings nevertheless remain a fundamental musical, compositional, and, at least for some, ethical problem cannot be denied: it will certainly continue to haunt both Handel scholars and other thoughtful musicians.[29] For if nothing else, many of Handel's sources, whatever their flaws, are too substantial, too attractive, and too rich with compositional implications to be dismissed as mere thematic springboards, or to be relegated to scholarly footnotes.[30] To grapple with this problem, and to extend the search for a better understanding of Handel's need to borrow, we must not only try to locate the remaining sources for Handel's borrowings (a task that may never be fully attained), but, equally important, we must also undertake a more detailed analytical study of Handel's sources, the use he made of them, and the precise role they play in his compositions. Only then shall we be in a position to gauge the true extent to which Handel met Johann Mattheson's famous stipulation, "Borrowing is permissible; but one must return the thing borrowed with interest, i.e., one must so construct and develop imitations that they are prettier and better than the pieces from which they are derived."[31]

NOTES

1. I wish to thank John Roberts, Timothy Jackson, and David Stern for reading an earlier version of this essay and making numerous helpful suggestions for changes, which have been incorporated in the present revision.
2. *Handel Sources: Materials for the Study of Handel's Borrowings*, ed. John H. Roberts, 9 vols. (New York: Garland Publishing, 1986–1988).
3. Ellwood Derr, "Handel's Procedures for Composing with Materials from Telemann's 'Harmonischer Gottes-Dienst' in 'Solomon'," and John H. Roberts, "Handel's Borrowings from Telemann: An Inventory," both in *Göttinger Händel-Beiträge*, vol. 1 (Kassel: Bärenreiter, 1984), pp. 116–146 and 147–171, respectively. Roberts provides a particularly vivid perspective on problems associated with Handel's borrowings during the eighteenth century in "Handel and Vinci's 'Didone abbandonata': Revisions and Borrowings," *Music and Letters*, 68, 2 (April 1987): 141–150.
4. *Hallische Händel-Ausgabe* (Kassel: Bärenreiter, 1955–), series IV, vol. 1 (1955, ed. Rudolf Steglich), pp. 22–23; this edition of Handel's works is referred to in succeeding notes as *HHA*.
5. A somewhat similar view is expressed in George J. Buelow's perceptive

historical survey, "The Case for Handel's Borrowings: The Judgment of Three Centuries," in *Handel Tercentenary Collection*, ed. Stanley Sadie and Anthony Hicks (London and Basingstoke: Macmillan; Ann Arbor, Mich.: UMI Research Press, 1987), p. 78.

6. Handel, *Georg Friedrich Händels Werke*, ed. Friedrich Chrysander (Leipzig: Breitkopf & Härtel, 1858–1894, 1902), vol. 28 (1868), pp. 135–138. This edition is referred to as the "Chrysander edition" in succeeding notes.

7. Georg Philipp Telemann, *Musikalische Werke* (Kassel: Bärenreiter, 1950–), vol. 14 (ed. Joh. Philipp Hinnenthal, 1963), p. 63; this edition is referred to as *Werke* in the notes that follow. Handel's borrowing from Telemann's E♭ Concerto is cited, as are all but the last example of borrowing presented in this paper, in Max Seiffert, "G. Ph. Telemann's 'Musique de table' als Quelle für Händel," *Bulletin de la Société "Union Musicologique*," 4, 1 (1924); see pp. 10 and 25–27. It is also cited in Pippa Drummond, *The German Concerto* (Oxford: Clarendon Press, 1980), pp. 175–176 and 357; in Roberts, "Inventory," p. 171, no. 126 (all the examples of borrowing discussed in the present paper are listed in Roberts, "Inventory"); and, along with invaluable historical information, in William D. Gudger, "The Organ Concertos of G. F. Handel: A Study Based on the Primary Sources" (Ph.D. diss., Yale University, 1973), vol. 1, pp. 243–248 and vol. 2, pp. 111–114.

8. Halfway through its opening movement (bars 57ff.), Handel borrows still more material form Telemann's opening group of passages (bars 12ff.), but a discussion of this second borrowing's considerable analytical implications must be reserved for another occasion.

9. For a thoughtful reexamination of Telemann's music see Nicholas Anderson, "Georg Philipp Telemann: A Tercentenary Reassessment," *Early Music*, 9, 4 (October 1981): 499–505. The most illuminating study of Telemann's orchestral music remains Siegfried Kross, *Das Instrumentalkonzert bei Georg Philipp Telemann* (Tutzing: Hans Schneider, 1969); see especially chapter 7, "Stilfragen im Instrumentalkonzert Telemanns."

10. *HHA*, series IV, vol. 15 (ed. Frederick Hudson, 1979), pp. 51–62 (the other works in vol. 15 were edited by Terence Best; see note 27, below).

11. Telemann, *Werke*, 12 (ed. Hinnenthal, 1959): 80–95.

12. A list of the correspondences between the Handel and Telemann Concerti is given in Roberts, "Inventory," p. 160, no. 57; see also Seiffert, "Quelle," pp. 10 and 19–21. It is rather ironic that William Boyce in turn borrowed from Handel's Concerto in one of his overtures; see Drummond, *The German Concerto*, pp. 178–179. According to Arnold Schering, the Concerto derives from Vivaldi's Violin Concerto in C, op. 8, no. 6, but this seems rather doubtful; see Schering, *Geschichte des*

Instrumentalkonzerts, 2nd ed. (Leipzig: Breitkopf & Härtel, 1927), p. 68.

13. Many Baroque ritornelli are marked by tripartite design; the important analytical ramifications of this division were suggested, if incipiently, in Wilhelm Fischer's classic study, "Zur Entwicklungsgeschichte des Wiener klassischen Stils," *Studien zur Musikwissenschaft*, vol. 3 (1915), pp. 32–33, and have more recently been usefully employed by both Pippa Drummond (*The German Concerto*, pp. 54–56 and passim) and Laurence Dreyfus ("J. S. Bach's Concerto Ritornellos and the Question of Invention," *The Musical Quarterly*, 71, 3 [1985]: 327–358; see especially pp. 329–330). In examples 9.3 and 9.4 the three parts of each ritornello are marked by the capital letters A, B and C.

14. Telemann's bars 15 and 21 are taken up by Handel only incidentally, in bars 15 and 17; bars 9–18—the third part of Handel's ritornello—are based on the second part, bars 7–10, of Telemann's ritornello.

15. I wish to thank David Stern for drawing my attention to the significance of the sectional enlargement.

16. To be sure, there are many compositions by Telemann that show a characteristically Baroque harmonic rhythm, and many Handel works that display a fundamentally slower harmonic rhythm; furthermore, the harmonic rhythm within any one piece tends to fluctuate, especially at major points of articulation, and to operate on different levels of structure. I have kept these considerations in mind while formulating my generalizations regarding stylistic matters in the Handel and Telemann concerto movements.

The complex network of relations between meter, rhythm, harmonic rhythm, and style is treated in some detail in Edward T. Cone's *Musical Form and Musical Performance* (New York: W. W. Norton, 1968), pp. 66–82 (see especially pp. 66, 72, and 79), and in Joel Lester, *The Rhythms of Tonal Music* (Carbondale, Ill.: Southern Illinois University Press, 1986), pp. 127–156 and passim. See also Mark DeVoto's observation regarding a Schenkerian approach to harmonic rhythm on different levels in the entry, "Harmonic Rhythm," in Don Randel, ed., the *New Harvard Dictionary of Music* (Cambridge, Mass.: Belknap Press, 1986), p. 364 (cf. Walter Piston, *Harmony*, 5th ed., revised and expanded by Mark DeVoto [New York: W. W. Norton, 1987], pp. 189–203). The manifestation of post-Baroque styles in Telemann's music is suggestively, if somewhat ambiguously, discussed in Richard Petzoldt, *George Philipp Telemann*, trans. Horace Fitzpatrick (New York: Oxford University Press, 1974), pp. 189–191, and, more concretely, in Martin Ruhnke's article on Telemann in *The New Grove Dictionary of Music and Musicians* (London: Macmillan, 1980), vol. 18, pp. 653–654, reprinted in *The New Grove North European Baroque Masters* (New York:

W. W. Norton, 1985), pp. 307–310; still more valuable observations are to be found in Drummond, *The German Concerto*, pp. 211–216, 228–229, and 237.

Other important studies of changes in compositional procedures during the emergence of the Classical and pre-Classical styles are William S. Newman, "Musical Form as a Generative Process," *Journal of Aesthetics and Art Criticism*, 12, 3 (March 1954): 301–309, and John Walter Hill, "The Anti-Galant Attitude of F. M. Veracini," in Hill, ed., *Studies in Musicology in Honor of Otto E. Albrecht* (Kassel: Bärenreiter, 1980), pp. 158–196; Hill's article contains substantial bibliographic and critical information on studies of the Galant style.

17. The unpredictable quality of successive motivic groups often obtains also in Telemann's accompanimental or developmental reuse of earlier material, tying in with Telemann's general tendency to generate additional intensity by employing textures characteristic of chamber music in the course of the Concerto's solo instrumental exchanges. Some intriguing ideas concerning the interdependence of motive and form in Telemann's concerti are expressed in Kross, *Instrumentalkonzert*, pp. 89–90.

18. Only during the final approach to the tonic do the soli enter the space of the tonic. It has become rather less fashionable to regard the concerto as a manifestation of conflict between the opposing forces of solo and tutti in recent years; see the illuminating observations in John A. Meyer, "The Idea of Conflict in the Concerto," *Studies in Music*, 8 (1974): 38–52, and in an earlier essay by Diana McVeagh, "The Concerto: Contest or Co-operation?" *Music and Letters*, 28, 2 (April 1947): 115–120. I nevertheless believe that Handel's soli and tutti are more than occasionally at odds with each other, their opposition having been carefully worked out by various elements of the design.

19. In this connection see the closing remarks in Derr, "Handel's Procedures," pp. 143–144.

20. Handel, Chrysander edition, 28: 118–123. The Concerto, a collection of posthumously assembled movements, is essentially in D minor, but the movement under discussion is in D major.

21. Telemann, *Werke*, 13 (ed. Hinnenthal, 1962): 17–27.

22. See Roberts, "Inventory," p. 171, no. 125; Seiffert, "Quelle," pp. 10 and 25–27; Drummond, *The German Concerto*, p. 356; and Gudger, "The Organ Concertos of G. F. Handel," 1:229–234 and 2:99–100. My discussion parallels Gudger's relatively detailed account at several points, though the conclusions I reach regarding Handel's style are somewhat different (cf. especially Gudger, 1:308).

23. Only differences between the Handel and Telemann works that affect larger issues of structure and style can be dealt with here. No more

than passing mention can thus be made of Handel's remarkable foreground changes, such as his replacement in bars 5–6 (and in corresponding measures) of Telemann's tonic-dominant alternation by a sequential series of descending parallel tenths, his replacement in bars 13–14 of Telemann's repetitive $^{6-5}_{4-3}$ alternations over the dominant (Telemann, bars 9–10) by a more sonorous tonic extension in which the part writing is characteristically varied upon repetition, his addition of motivically rising arpeggios to the bass figurations throughout, and his substantially richer part writing (quite apparent in the present two-stave reduction of the score, which despite its brevity helps throw the artistically molded shape of Handel's inner voices into relief). Handel's simplification of Telemann's bass line in bars 1–2, however, is far-reaching in its implications and is dealt with later in the essay.

24. A composer such as J. S. Bach, by contrast, was careful to preserve the rhythmic implications of his thematic material even when using it as accompaniment (see, for instance, the opening movements of the Clavier Concerto in D minor, the Violin Concerto in E major, and the Fifth Brandenburg Concerto).

25. Handel, Chrysander edition, 26 (1867): 207–212.

26. Telemann, *Werke*, 13 (ed. Hinnenthal, 1962): 83–99.

27. Winton Dean, *Handel's Dramatic Oratorios and Masques* (London: Oxford University Press, 1959), pp. 523, 532, and Roberts, "Inventory," pp. 150–151 and p. 169, no. 116; the borrowing from Telemann was first cited by Roberts in "Inventory." Porta's *Numitore* has recently been published in *Handel Sources* (see note 2, above), vol. 4; the Aria from which Handel borrowed is found on pp. 22–23 (cf. the *Introduction*, pp. xiii–xiv). The Overture for two clarinets has been published in *HHA*, series IV, vol. 15 (1979, ed. Terence Best); see pp. 90–91.

28. Such interdependence of borrowings at different levels of structure is emblematic of the great sophistication and complexity of Handel's compositional method. The admixture of borrowings from different compositions and different composers was, however, standard procedure with him; see Roberts, "Inventory," p. 150.

29. Valuable remarks regarding moral issues in Handel's borrowings are found in Stanley Sadie's review of *Handel Sources* in *Early Music*, 17, 1 (February 1989): 103–106; see especially 105–106.

30. John Roberts has recently made a convincing case for attributing the reason for Handel's borrowings to difficulties with melodic invention; see Roberts, "Why Did Handel Borrow," in *Handel Tercentenary Collection* (cited in note 5, above), pp. 83–92.

31. Johann Mattheson, *Der volkommene Capellmeister*, revised translation with critical commentary by Ernest C. Harriss (Ann Arbor: UMI Research Press, 1981), p. 298.